D1739202

The School *of* Antioch

BIBLE IN THE CHRISTIAN ORTHODOX TRADITION

Vahan S. Hovhanessian
General Editor

Vol. 6

This book is a volume in a Peter Lang monograph series.
Every volume is peer reviewed and meets
the highest quality standards for content and production.

PETER LANG
New York • Bern • Frankfurt • Berlin
Brussels • Vienna • Oxford • Warsaw

The School *of* Antioch

Biblical Theology and the Church in Syria

Edited by
Vahan S. Hovhanessian

PETER LANG
New York • Bern • Frankfurt • Berlin
Brussels • Vienna • Oxford • Warsaw

Library of Congress Cataloging-in-Publication Data

The School of Antioch: biblical theology and the church in Syria /
edited by Vahan S. Hovhanessian.
pages cm. — (Bible in the Christian Orthodox tradition; Vol. 6)
Includes bibliographical references and index.
1. Bible—Criticism, interpretation, etc.—History. 2. Bible—Hermeneutics.
3. Antiochian school. 4. John Chrysostom, Saint, –407.
5. Theodoret, Bishop of Cyrrhus. 6. Theodore, Bishop of Mopsuestia,
approximately 350–428 or 429. I. Hovhanessian, Vahan, editor.
BS483.3.S346   230'.14—dc23   2015009645
ISBN 978-1-4331-2806-6 (hardcover)
ISBN 978-1-4539-1550-9 (e-book)
ISSN 1947-5977

Bibliographic information published by **Die Deutsche Nationalbibliothek**.
Die Deutsche Nationalbibliothek lists this publication in the "Deutsche
Nationalbibliografie"; detailed bibliographic data are available
on the Internet at http://dnb.d-nb.de/.

Contents

Acknowledgments

Members of the unit "Bible in the Eastern and Oriental Orthodox Traditions" of the *Society of Biblical Literature* (SBL) are happy to present this book into the hands of scholars and students of biblical studies, as a new volume in the series "Bible in the Christian Orthodox Tradition" of the Peter Lang International Academic Publishers.

As in the previous volumes of the series, this book offers the latest scholoarly findings and conclusions in the field of biblical theology and research from the perspective, and based on the traditions, of the hisrtocial Orthoox Churches which read, studied, taught and commented on the Bible in their native languages. In this volume we focus on the biblical hermeneutics, criticism, interpretation and theology of the Church of Antioch: the Church that was born and nurtured in the historical Roman province of Syria-Palestina.

Thanks are due to all the scholars who contributed to this volume. Special thanks to Professor Paul Nadim Tarazi for his contribution to this volume and for being the inspiration behind the creation and continuation of our SBL group.

As the objective of our SBL unit is, may this volume function as a bridge introducing contemporary readers to the richness of the biblical theology of the centuries-old Churches of the East, the majority of whose theological literature remains unearthed until today. At the same time, may it be an opportutnity to invite scholars to explore the interpretive, hermenutical and exegetical tools used by these churches and to incorporate them into the contemporary critical approaches of biblical criticism.

+Vahan S. Hovhanessian, PhD
Series Editor

Abbreviations

AoF	Altorientalische Forschungen
AsMaj	Asia Major: Third Series
AWLMJ	Akademie der Wissenschaften und der Literatur in Mainz
JA	Journal asiatique,
NKGWG	Nachrichten von der Gesellschaft der Wissenschaften zu Göttingen. Philologisch-historische Klasse
OCP	Orientalia Christiana Periodica
OstStud	Ostkirchliche Studien
PBA	Proceedings of the British Academy
ROC	La revue de l'orient chrétien
SBL	Society for Biblical Literature
SPAW	Sitzungsberichte der preussischen Akademie der Wissenschaften
UAJ	Ural-altaische Jahrbücher
WJKP	Westminster John Knox Press
ZDMG	Zeitschrift der Deutschen Morgenlandischen Gesellschaft

Introduction

The essays in this volume on *The Bible in the Orthodox Tradition* reflect the principles and perspectives of the "school" of Antioch (4th-5th centuries). A brief summary of contemporary scholarship on Antiochian[1] heremeneutics will provide the context for the collection of essays that appear in this volume.

Since the early 1990s, there has been a rising interest in Antiochene exegesis among biblical and patristic scholars. Brevard Childs observed the motivations and issues that have driven scholars to revise their understanding of Antiochian exegesis:

> Particularly misleading in reference to the Antiochenes has been the contrast between the spiritual concerns of the Alexandrians and the historical concerns of the Antiochenes. Recent scholarship, summarized by Bradley Nassif in 1993 ("The Spiritual Exegesis of Scripture"), has therefore focused on the 'spiritual' exegesis of Scripture in the school of the Antiochenes. The crucial term around which the debate has revolved is the term θεωρία, the spiritual hermeneutic at whose center lies the dual concern for both the historical and a Christological reading of the Bible."[2]

The 1993 article to which Childs refers was subsequently updated in my essay "'Spiritual Exegesis' in the School of Antioch" in *New Perspectives on Historical Theology: Essays in Memory of John Meyendorff.*[3] That essay summarizes the contributions of only nine scholars (up to 1996) who had written on this subject over the past century, and critiques the secondary literature in which the Antiochian θεωρία (*theoria*) appears. I concluded it by identifying six areas for future research on Antiochian θεωρία. I summarize them here to provide direction to the ongoing work of modern-day students and scholars who might wish to take up this much needed area of research. The first and sixth items in the following list are currently underway, but the rest remains to be done in a doctor's or master's thesis:

1. Conduct separate monographs on individual Antiochian authors.

2. See to what extent, if any, the term θεωρία was used as part of the technical vocabulary of the rhetorical schools. If so, what influence did those schools have on the use of θεωρία in patristic exegesis?

3. Discover the extent to which Syriac exegetical literature employed θεωρία. Examine if and how Theodore of Mopsuestia's and John Chrysostom's use of θεωρία influenced Syriac exegesis. Theodore's writings survive only in Syriac translations.

4. Explore the extent (if any) to which the messianic exegesis of the Antiochian writers influenced Irish exegesis from the seventh to twelfth centuries. Irish exegesis was heavily Antiochian in its approach.

5. Trace the influence and continuities between the Antiochian's use of θεωρία in messianic exegesis and the works of Thomas Aquinas and Nicholas of Lyria. Similarly, scholars may wish to discover the patristic origins and parallel exegetical patterns between the Antiochian authors and the christological exegesis and pneumatology of the Reformers and later Protestant scholastics.

6. Determine the extent to which θεωρία may enrich the interpretive methods and hermeneutical theories of contemporary biblical scholars.

I have summarized the essential points of my earlier doctoral dissertation on "Antiochene Θεωρία in John Chrysostom's Exegesis" in *The Bible in the Eastern and Oriental Orthodox Churches*.[4] Dr. Rick Perhai, a contributor to the present volume, has sought to advance that work in his recent doctoral dissertation titled *Antiochene Theoria in the Commentaries of Theodore of Mopsuestia and Theodoret of Cyrus*. Future research will benefit considerably from the advances he has made not only in the works of Theodore and Theodoret, but in the contemporary relevance of Antiochian Θεωρία for biblical exegesis today.

The other essays in this volume lead us to ask, "Is there really a unified approach to biblical exegesis that we can properly call an Antiochian 'school'? If so, who comprises this 'school' and what does it look like, hermeneutically and exegetically?" Perhai answers these questions at length in chapters 2 and 3 of his dissertation, noting the works of scholars involved in the debate. He maintains that there is, in fact, a collective group of authors that we can legitimately call "Antiochian," and that their common approach to biblical interpretation is sufficiently unified as to justify their work as a "school" of hermeneutical thought. Others, such as Donald Fairbairn, in his book *Grace and Christology in the Early Church*, disagree noting that the idea of a so-called Antiochian "school" was not invented until the 19th century. Antiochian authors are united neither by "literal" exegesis nor by a particular Christology. Fairbairn sees more differences between the authors of the so-called Antiochian "school" than there are similarities.[5] Thus, the nature of "unity and diversity" in Antioch exegesis is now front and center as never before in the history of scholarship.[6]

The current state of the field, broadly outlined above, highlights the importance of the other essays in this present volume on *The Bible in the Orthodox Tradition*. The essay by Paul Tarazi titled "Exegesis for John Chrysostom: Preaching and Teaching the Bible" emphasizes the centrality of Scripture in the life of the church, then as now. Tarazi does not want us simply to repeat the same methods and conclusions of Chrysostom's exegesis. Rather, he wishes to encourage his legacy as an interpreter of biblical texts. A close study of Chrysostom's understanding of the task of exegesis encourages us to carry on the Orthodox tradition by engaging in the creative enterprise of contemporary historical-critical methods of exegesis. Just as Chrysostom employed the methods and tasks of the rhetorical schools in Christian antiquity in the service of preaching and teaching, so we must also preach and teach the Bible using all the tools and techniques available to us today.

The essay by Michael Azar tackles the thorny question of "John Chrysostom and the Johannine Jews." Azar challenges commonly held views and extends the contributions of Robert Wilken's masterful studies on *John Chrysostom and the Jews. Rhetoric and Reality in the Late 4th Century;* and *Jews and Christians in Antioch in the First Four Centuries of the Common Era.*[7] Vahan S. Hovhanessian, a scholar of Biblical and Armenian studies, explores "The Commentary of St. Ephrem on the Apocryphal Third Corinthians." This is an original analysis of a neglected text in the Antiochian tradition. As such it widens our comprehension of the diversity of Antiochian exegesis and its approach to biblical interpretation. Mark Dickens likewise breaks new ground in his essay on "Biblical Fragments from the Christian Library of Turfan, an Eastern Outpost of the Antiochian Tradition." The Library of Turfan houses some 900 manuscripts in Syriac, Christian Soghdian and Christian Old Turkic, as well as New Persian that were found in the opening decade of the twentieth century at a monastery near Bulayiq, Turfan. Here again we find an exciting new contribution to our growing body of knowledge on Antiochian exegesis.

The collective contributions of the essays in this volume provide us with new and exciting advances in our knowledge of the Antiochian tradition of exegesis. But they do much more than that. They remind us that the ultimate purpose of exegesis is not the mere acquisition of knowledge. Rather, the ultimate task of exegesis is to lead us into to a living relationship with the divine Person about whom the Scriptures speak: Jesus Christ, the risen Lord and Savior of the world.

Exegesis for John Chrysostom:
Preaching and Teaching the Bible

A ny serious discussion of the Antiochean School of biblical exegesis cannot circumvent the great contribution of St John Chrysostom through his commentaries and theological writings. A discussion pertaining to St John Chrysostom, however, cannot avoid dealing with Holy Scripture and its place in the domain that has come to be commonly known as theology. My contention in this paper is that this father of the church presented us with a paradigm which, if followed, will bring a solution to two dilemmas that have plagued the life of the church for centuries. It will bring an end to the tension extant in all Christian traditions between theologians and students of the church fathers, on the one hand, and biblical scholars, on the other hand. It will also help bridge the gap, shown time and again to have been unnecessary, between the Eastern and Oriental Orthodox Churches.

Scripture and Theology

However one looks at it, the apparent impasse created between theologians, on the one hand, and biblical scholars, on the other hand, boils down to the following question: Is the Bible simply one of many early exercises in theological discourse? Theologians are forced to answer this question in the affirmative. To do otherwise would (1) void scripture of any value for their particular field of interest, and (2) contradict the stance of early Christian writers who always quoted scripture and came themselves to be considered normative. Such an approach, however, ultimately does void scripture of its authority, since it makes of it a mere beginning for a continual discourse that would be carried out through the centuries.

To be sure, the term "beginning" entails some level of honor. Yet it is an honor that relegates the honoree to the low level of a "modest" beginner who opens the path toward the glorious present—a present associated with the work of the contemporary generation which, of course, includes us. Such an honor bestowed upon the person of the initiator is actually a respectful way to dismiss his or her value for the present day. After all, with unavoidable advances of any human discourse, one is bound to keep only what is deemed still relevant and to discard the rest. Take, for example, the case of Hippocrates in the field of medicine. He is hailed as the "father of medicine," yet his importance is relegated to a time past. The outcome is that it is modern physicians who honor him and give him importance, in that his value was for his own time.

The same applies, *de facto*, to any human discourse, and the theological one is no exception. Consider, for instance, how we are used to saying that the accepted terminology of scripture is understood according to the faith of Nicea; the latter is clarified in Chalcedon for the Chalcedonians; the Cappadocians vindicate Athanasius; Maximus explicates and brings to further fruition the teachings of his predecessors. It is as though every generation not only elucidates, but actually "pushes ahead" the teaching of the previous one by extracting the fruit inherent in the seed. This is clearly a far cry from Paul's approach to the authority of scripture. His classic "as it is written" (καθὼς γέγραπται) was never meant to be an elucidation of what scripture is saying; rather it is an appeal to the undisputed authority of scripture. For him, scripture is not a *first* word needing clarification or development; rather, it is the *last* word in the matter at hand and of every matter at hand dealt with in scripture. Paul did not "push ahead" the teaching of the Old Testament by bringing more light to it and by inviting his hearers to understand it in the light of *his* teaching. Rather, he read and judged his contemporary situation in the light of the Old Testament authoritative teaching.

What about the biblical scholars since the Renaissance and the Reformation? Generally, they fare better only in the sense that their field of inquiry is, or at least is supposed to be, scripture. They fall, however, into the same trap. Three striking examples should suffice. Martin Luther not only commended his friend Phillip Melanchton on the latter's theological work, *Loci Communes*, but he himself wrote on the two natures of Christ. Besides his valuable commentaries, John Calvin's major work is his theological *summa* "Institutions of the Christian Religion." One of the more influential works of another eminent Protestant exegete of the last century, Rudolf Bultmann, is his *Theology of the New Testament*. His case is telling since he repeatedly asserts that the Bible is not "a word *about* (concerning) God" but God's word in the sense of "a word *from* God."[1]

The 20th century saw biblical scholars producing many colossal works entitled *Theology of the Old Testament* as well as *Theology of the New Testament*. The intention, to be sure, was to underline the primacy of the Bible in any theological endeavor; still the titles betrayed the underlying reality that the Bible was indeed a "theological" endeavor as opposed to a historicizing, descriptive one. The factual result was that these scholars viewed themselves as the heirs of the prophets and apostles and thought they could bring a high level of fruition to the intellectual discourse started by the Prophets and Apostles. To my mind, this way of perceiving matters is none other than the Hegelian view that controlled not only theology from the beginning of the 19th century, but also philosophy and the writing of history as well. An example of this influence is the approach to world history predominant among British and then U.S. historians and politicians, who view their own time and country as being the end which previous world history converges and culminates into, and that their own commonwealth is the paradigm to be sought after by the rest of the world communities.[2]

In spite of all appearances, this is not a new phenomenon. It did not originate with Hegel; he just sanctified it. This approach actually originated in Athens, was then taken over by imperial Rome, then by imperial Constantinople—the new Rome, and then by Charlemagne. Each of those societies saw itself as the highest expression of human civilization.

The Way Out of the Impasse

Is there a way out of this impasse which theological discourse has thrown us into so deeply? Even the Protestant Reformation, with all its ado about the return to the primacy of the Bible, was not able to disentangle itself from its tight hold. Every new generation tries to find the solution in a new "approach," hailing it as the right way to interpret the biblical text. Yet every such endeavor is *a priori* doomed, since it is looking for a "theological" key. It is as though the Bible needs a Hermes, a divine emissary, thus *another* god, with a device to unlock the divine message.

The intrinsic inappropriateness of all theological endeavors lies in the fact that a central teaching—if not the ultimate premise of the Bible—is that there is only *one* God who *has already fully spoken*. His "word" (λόγος) is totally behind us, and to imagine that we can develop it through hermeneutics, i.e., by doing the work of Hermes, is sheer blasphemy since we would be contravening the first commandment. Furthermore, this divine word which is behind us has also been *fully committed into writing* for all subsequent ages. Finally, this divine word, which took form (to use the theological terminology, was incarnate) in writing (ἔχοντα τὴν μόρφωσιν τῆς γνώσεως καὶ τῆς ἀληθείας ἐν τῷ νόμῳ|; Rom 2:20) is the same divine word that had been uttered orally and was refused. Actually it was committed in writing in spite—actually, because—of having been refused in order to make it clear that it stands for all ages as it was delivered, without any possibility of addition or subtraction of any kind or sort. This reality stands forever as a light at the end of the tunnel of our impasse, and this is what Chrysostom fully and correctly understood. So let me first give room to scripture itself and then to our honoree in this paper.

Scripture: The Written and Solely Valid Divine Word

I shall confine myself to the three clearest passages in the Old Testament and one New Testament passage, all of which reflect the points I just made concerning the divine word. The first passage is Ezekiel (Ezek 2:9-10) where we are told that the prophet is handed a fully written message to which nothing can be added and which the addressees are going to refuse just as their fathers did before them (vv.3-7):

> And he said to me, "Son of man, I send you to the people of Israel, to a nation of rebels, who have rebelled against me; they and their fathers have transgressed against me to this very day. The people also are impudent and stubborn: I send you to them; and you shall say to them, 'Thus says the Lord God.' And whether they hear or refuse to hear (for they are a rebellious house) they will know that there has been a prophet among them. And

you, son of man, be not afraid of them, nor be afraid of their words, though briers and thorns are with you and you sit upon scorpions; be not afraid of their words, nor be dismayed at their looks, for they are a rebellious house. And you shall speak my words to them, whether they hear or refuse to hear; for they are a rebellious house. But you, son of man, hear what I say to you; be not rebellious like that rebellious house; open your mouth, and eat what I give you." And when I looked, behold, a hand was stretched out to me, and, lo, a written scroll was in it; and he spread it before me; and it had writing on the front and on the back, and there were written on it words of lamentation and mourning and woe. (Ezek 2:3-10)

The second passage is from Jeremiah, and here the importance of the written word is more telling since, in this case, the latest canonical version is actually a repetition of an earlier *scroll*:

Now, after the king had burned the scroll with the words which Baruch wrote at Jeremiah's dictation, the word of the Lord came to Jeremiah: "Take another scroll and write on it all the former words that were in the first scroll, which Jehoiakim the king of Judah has burned..." Then Jeremiah took another scroll and gave it to Baruch the scribe, the son of Neriah, who wrote on it at the dictation of Jeremiah all the words of the scroll which Jehoiakim king of Judah had burned in the fire; and many similar words were added to them. (Jer 36:27-28, 32)[3]

The third passage is from Deuteronomy and is a second issuance at Mount Nebo of the written Law promulgated at Sinai/Horeb, which reflects the approach of the Jeremian school:[4]

And you shall again obey the voice of the Lord, and keep all his commandments which I command you this day. The Lord your God will make you abundantly prosperous in all the work of your hand, in the fruit of your body, and in the fruit of your cattle, and in the fruit of your ground; for the Lord will again take delight in prospering you, as he took delight in your fathers, if you obey the voice of the Lord your God, to keep his commandments and his statutes *which are written in this book of the law*, if you turn to the Lord your God with all your heart and with all your soul. For this commandment which I command you this day is not too hard for you, neither is it far off. It is not in heaven, that you should say, "Who will go up for us to heaven, and bring it to us, that we may hear it and do it?" Neither is it beyond the sea, that you should say, "Who will go over the sea for us, and bring it to us, that we may hear it and do it?" *But the word is very near you; it is in your mouth and in your heart, so that you can do it.* See, I have set before you this day life and good, death and evil. (Deut 30:8-15)

The passage in the New Testament which mimics Deuteronomy and thus makes it clear that New Testament literature was patterned after Old Testament writings is found in Galatians, arguably the first New Testament document:

> But even if we, or an angel from heaven, should preach to you a gospel contrary to that which we preached to you, let him be accursed. *As we have said before, so now I say again*, If any one is preaching to you a gospel contrary to that which you received, let him be accursed. (Gal 1:8-9)

Paul's *oral* teaching to the Galatians, which they refused, was none other than what was consigned in his letter to them. To imagine that this teaching was floating about in an oral form in Galatia and was picked up by the following generations flatly contradicts the fact that those who had originally heard Paul's message refused or at least perverted it (v.7).[5] Actually, had that generation accepted the Pauline gospel in the first place, we probably would not have had that letter at hand and consequently would have run the risk of receiving a perverted form of that gospel centuries later.

Chrysostom's View of Scripture

That this view of scripture was fully perceived and endorsed by Chrysostom is evident in his first homily on Matthew:

> It were indeed meet for us not at all to require the aid of the written Word, but to exhibit a life so pure, that the grace of the Spirit should be instead of books to our souls, and that as these are inscribed with ink, even so should our hearts be with the Spirit. But, since we have utterly put away from us this grace, come, let us at any rate embrace the second best course. For that the former was better, God hath made manifest, both by His words, and by His doings. Since unto Noah, and unto Abraham, and unto his offspring, and unto Job, and unto Moses too, He discoursed not by writings, but Himself by Himself, finding their mind pure. But after the whole people of the Hebrews had fallen into the very pit of wickedness, then and thereafter was a written word, and tables, and the admonition which is given by these. And this one may perceive was the case, not of the saints in the Old Testament only, but also of those in the New. For neither to the apostles did God give anything in writing, but instead of written words, He promised that He would give them the grace of the Spirit: for "He," saith our Lord, "shall bring all things to your remembrance." And that thou mayest learn that this was far better, hear what He saith by the Prophet: "I will make a new covenant with you, putting my laws into their mind, and in their heart I will write them," and, "they shall be all taught of God." And Paul too, pointing out the same superiority, said, that they had received a law "not in tables of

stone, but in fleshy tables of the heart."

But since in process of time they made shipwreck, some with regard to doctrines, others as to life and manners, there was again need that they should be put in remembrance by the written word. Reflect then how great an evil it is for us, who ought to live so purely as not even to need written words, but to yield up our hearts, as books, to the Spirit; now that we have lost that honor, and are come to have need of these, to fail again in duly employing even this second remedy. For if it be a blame to stand in need of written words, and not to have brought down on ourselves the grace of the Spirit; consider how heavy the charge of not choosing to profit even after this assistance, but rather treating what is written with neglect, as if it were cast forth without purpose, and at random, and so bringing down upon ourselves our punishment with increase. But that no such effect may ensue, let us give strict heed unto the things that are written; and let us learn how the Old Law was given on the one hand, how on the other the New Covenant.[6]

It is then no wonder that this father of the church is de facto dismissed from works that discuss the development of theology during the fourth century, its golden age. He is dismissed, we are told, because he did not engage in theological discourse and thus did not promote it. But he obviously had a very valid reason. He understood that God's word is to be channeled to every new generation as it stands in its written form,[7] not for the people to comprehend; actually it is very clear. Rather, it is for the people *to do*[8]—it is instruction and the people are stubbornly refusing to heed it! This word, thus scripture, is not a mental proposition about God and his activity; rather it is ordinances, commandments, and statutes to be observed. Let me quote Chrysostom himself:

Some people, out of restless curiosity, want to elaborate idly and irresponsibly doctrines which are of no benefit to those who understand them, or else are actually incomprehensible. Others call God to account for his judgments and struggle to measure the great deep. For the Psalmist says: "Thy judgments are a great deep." You will find that few are deeply concerned about faith and conduct, but the majority go in for these elaborate theories and investigate questions to which there is no answer and whose very investigation rouses God's anger. For when we struggle to learn things which God himself did not will us to know, we shall never succeed—how can we, against God's will?—and we shall gain nothing but our own peril from the investigation.[9]

My assessment of how Chrysostom is generally viewed in Books of Dogmatic Theology and Patristics is shared by Fr Philotheos Faros,

Professor of Pastoral Theology at Holy Cross Greek Orthodox School
of Theology (1969-76), who writes:

> It seems that St. John Chrysostom is a source of embarrassment for many
> modern Orthodox theologians . They either avoid him or have a conde-
> scending attitude towards him because he appears too practical to appeal to
> their scholarly tastes.
>
> In that sense, St. John Chrysostom's legacy could be critical of contempo-
> rary Orthodox ecclesiastical life, which seems to be enclosed between a
> scholastic theology, often lofty and sublime, but unable to contribute to the
> improvement and appropriate formation of ecclesiastical life, and an eccle-
> siastical practice crude and alien to the nature of the *Ekklesia* whose essence
> it distorts and deforms.
>
> It is very difficult if not impossible to scholasticize John Chrysostom's
> word because of its immediacy and direct contact with experience. Of
> course, it is not only the word of Chrysostom which is the product of eccle-
> siastical life. All the fathers of the Eastern Church were pastors. None of
> them was a scholastic... [However,] The difference between Chrysostom
> and most of the other Church fathers is that Chrysostom deals with the ex-
> perience of the common person. This gives to his theological word a unique
> value for our ecclesiastical life today because it can decisively influence its
> appropriate formation and development. A sublime and lofty theological
> word that does not correspond to our experience is not only not beneficial,
> but is disorienting, confusing, and it can be very easily used as an escape
> because it is not truthful.[10]

Thus Chrysostom essentially was not a "theologian," nor even an
"exegete" in the strict sense of the term, as e.g. Theodore of
Mopsuestia was. He was a preacher and teacher. To say that he was
unable to rise to high levels of mental discourse would be a cheap way
out of confessing that he presents us with a real challenge. Chrysostom, whom Libanius himself wanted as his successor,[11] took seriously
the reality of scripture: scripture is the message of fatherly corrective
instruction from someone whose basic function is that of a *judge*. This
reality that God is primarily and essentially judge, is the premise and
consequently the key that unlocks all the seemingly difficult biblical
texts. It is the crimson thread that holds all scripture together—the
New Testament as well as the Old Testament—and makes sense of it
at every turn of the page. Indeed, as early as Genesis 2-3 this is so.
And when the sin of Israel against God is subsumed in the people's re-
fusal to accept him as their sole king, it is because the king is essentially a judge. Suffice it to mention the case of King Solomon. Upon

requesting wisdom to discern between good and evil, instead of riches (1 Kg 3:9), Solomon's one and only test is a straightforward one: an act of judgment (vv.16-28). At the end of the story of his success as a judge in solving equitably the difficult case of establishing who was the child's mother, we hear: "And all Israel heard of the judgment which the king had rendered; and they stood in awe of the king, *because they perceived that the wisdom of God was in him, to render justice.*" (v.28)

So the biblical God's kingdom is not a matter of "theology" that figures out whether the mystery of that kingdom is a spiritual reality or an earthly reality. In spite of all appearances to the contrary, it is a metaphor to indicate that God, as king, will be the final judge. The Book of Daniel makes this amply clear—it culminates with God's final judgment, at which point the book is ordered to be sealed (12:1-5).

Another clear example is the Book of Isaiah. After the introductory chapter 1, which is quintessentially a judgment passage, Isaiah 2 describes the heavenly Jerusalem as being the city of God's teaching and *torah* where God's "light" is none other than the "fire" with which he judges his own people. This is precisely why, from that same throne, high and uplifted, God summons Isaiah and sends him to inform the people of his divine decision to fully bring to naught the sinful kingdom of Judah:

> And he said, "Go, and say to this people: 'Hear and hear, but do not understand; see and see, but do not perceive.' Make the heart of this people fat, and their ears heavy, and shut their eyes; lest they see with their eyes, and hear with their ears, and understand with their hearts, and turn and be healed." Then I said, "How long, O Lord?" And he said: "Until cities lie waste without inhabitant, and houses without men, and the land is utterly desolate, and the Lord removes men far away, and the forsaken places are many in the midst of the land. And though a tenth remain in it, it will be burned again, like a terebinth or an oak, whose stump remains standing when it is felled." (6:9-13)

The reason I illustrate the Book of Isaiah is because it allows me to show how Chrysostom correctly perceived the biblical text. In his comments on the opening verses of ch.6, Chrysostom does not delve, as often theologians do, into a fruitless discussion about "Isaiah's vision of God." Rather he captures the meaning of the text by reading it functionally, i.e., according to its intention:

"I saw the Lord seated." Christ has indeed said, "No one has seen God at any time. The only-begotten Son, who is in the bosom of the Father, has explained him.".... How then can Isaiah claim to have seen the Lord?... After all, no one has observed bare divinity in its pure essence except the only-begotten. Isaiah, on the other hand, claimed to have seen his power. It is impossible to see God in and of himself. Isaiah saw God in an assumed form, one as much lowered as Isaiah's weakness was elevated. That neither he nor anybody else has seen bare divinity is made very clear by what they claim. For example, Isaiah says, "I saw the Lord seated." But God does not sit. He does not have a bodily form. Not only does he say "Seated," but "Seated on a throne.".... Isaiah says, "I saw the Lord seated." But God does not sit. He does not have a bodily form. Not only does he say "Seated," but "Seated on a throne.".... Therefore, why does he now appear seated on a throne among the Seraphim? He is imitating a human custom because his message is to humans. For he is about to carry out a decision that involves great matters and the whole world, but which also concerns Jerusalem. For it was the custom of their judges not to work in secret but while seated on high platforms with curtains drawn while everyone stood. God, in imitation of these things, places the Seraphim about him, sits on a high throne, and pronounces his verdict from there. I will try to make this point from another prophet so that you will not regard my analysis with suspicion but understand that this really is God's way of revealing himself...[12] we can, as I said, deal with the question at hand accurately and explain the genre of each text. Therefore, why did he say, "I saw the Lord seated?" Sitting on a throne is always a symbol of judgment, as David said, "You have sat on the throne to judge righteously." ... His precise language makes it clear that he is not talking about a chair... To sit on the throne is to judge.[13]

However, as I indicated earlier, God behaves as a father instructing his children in the way to live in order to inherit his kingdom. And this is precisely what the *torah* is all about: the eschatological covenant (Mt 5-7) as well as that of the earlier Pentateuchal covenant. In both cases, those who do not live according to God's instruction shall not inherit his kingdom (Mt 7:21-27; Gal 5:19-21; 1 Cor 6:9-10).[14] Thus, scripture is not the judgment (except when it is on previous generations, i.e., a past judgment with the intention to educate). Rather, scripture, functionally, is a graceful "condescension" (συγκατάβασις) on God's part. This condescension, however, is not only material but also formal. God is educating his children in a way they can understand, that is, through the language of metaphor and not though complicated philosophical jargon that only a few elect can fathom. The intention for this is twofold: first, that the children understand and be found righteous on judgment day, and secondly, that on that day it be understood that "thou [God] art justified in thy sentence and blameless in thy judgment" as the Psalmist declares and the Apostle asserts (Ps 51:4b; Rom 3:4b). There is no way to avoid the ultimate and final judgment. This is precisely what Chrysostom understood, and he spent his life "communicating" the already clear biblical message to those who were in his charge, lovingly but sternly, as a true father would, understanding that all will be judged. As the student of Paul par excellence, he could not have missed his teacher's injunctions:

> For this reason I bow my knees before the Father, from whom every family (πατριά) in heaven and on earth is named... Fathers, do not provoke your children to anger, but bring them up in the discipline and instruction of the Lord... Masters, do the same to them, and forbear threatening, knowing that he who is both their Master and yours is in heaven, and that there is no partiality with him. (Eph 3:14-15; 6:4, 9)

Put otherwise, Chrysostom was extremely careful in both his sternness and love because he was the teacher who was preparing his students for the final test that someone else would be administering. Consequently and intentionally there was not much difference between his commentaries (on Galatians and on Isaiah 1-8) and his homilies. In both cases scripture was handled in a way that corresponds to what it really is: an instructional address from God to his people in preparation for the test lying ahead—not a theological treatise of some kind (as later many inferred, especially in regard to the letter to the Romans). And, as is clear from the entire scripture, and especially from the Gospel of Matthew, that test will not be on the correctness of creedal formulae and their meaning, but rather on whether or not one will have done God's will.[15]

Although Chrysostom proved to be the unchallenged master in this field, his attitude was not unique and was shared with a good number of fathers in the same geographical region of the Roman province of Syria, including Cyril of Jerusalem and Ephrem the Syrian. Their interest was quite different from that of the "Theological School" of Alexandria. Due to the philosophical mood of this city connected with the Royal Library, Christian teaching in Alexandria was drawn, through Philo's influence, into a "philosophical" discourse à la Plato and later à la Plotinus. Instead of remaining basically an exhortation (the scriptural para,klhsij and paramuqi,a) unto living the Christian life as was mainly the case in Syria, instead of following the Lord's injunction to teach the divine *torah* to all upcoming generations,[16] instead of making of themselves disciples in the scriptural "way" (of behavior), the Alexandrians entered into a debate with the Hellenes to convince them of the intellectual superiority of this new "philosophy." By doing so, they transposed the practical "truth of the gospel" (Gal 2:5, 14) as table fellowship under the aegis of the will of the one God[17] into an intellectual system of "philosophical" truth. The λόγος of instruction and healing was transformed into a philosophical λόγος to be debated. This is a far cry from Chrysostom's handling of the true scriptural λόγος:

> It is not the management of corn and barley, oxen or sheep, that is now under our consideration, nor any such like matters, but the very body of Jesus. For the Church of Christ, according to Saint Paul, is Christ's body, and he who is entrusted with its care ought to train it up to a state of healthiness, and beauty unspeakable, and to look everywhere, lest any spot or wrinkle, or other like blemish should mar its vigor and comeliness. For what is this but to make it appear worthy, so far as human power can, of the incorruptible and ever-blessed head which is set over it? If they who are ambitious of reaching an athletic condition of body need the help of physicians and trainers, and exact diet, and constant exercise, and a thousand other rules (for the omission of the merest trifle upsets and spoils the whole), how shall they to whose lot falls the care of the body, which has its conflict not against flesh and blood, but against powers unseen, be able to keep it sound and healthy, unless they far surpass ordinary human virtue, and are versed in all healing proper for the soul? Pray art thou not aware that that body is subject to more diseases and assaults that this flesh of ours, is more quickly corrupted, and more slow to recover? And by those who have the healing of these bodies, divers medicines have been discovered, and an apparatus of different instruments, and diet suitable for the sick; and often the condition of the atmosphere is of itself enough for the recovery of a sick man; and there are instances of seasonable sleep having saved the physician all further labor. But in the case before us, it is impossible to take any of these things into consideration; nay there is but one method and way of healing appointed, after we have gone wrong, and that is, *the powerful application of the word.*[18] *This is the one instrument the only diet, the finest atmosphere.* This takes the place of physic, cautery and cutting, and if it be needful to sear and amputate, this is the means which we must use, and if this be of no avail, all else is wasted; with this we both rouse the soul when it sleeps, and reduce it when it is inflamed; with this we cut off excesses, and fill up defect, and perform all manner of other operations which are requisite for the soul's health.[19]

The intimate connection between Alexandria, the city of knowledge, and Rome[20] forced the continuation of the philosophical debate into the new Rome. This explains the theologico-political axis between Alexandria and Constantinople that developed during and after the Constantinian era. Thus began the intra-Christian persecutions between Niceans (Orthodox) and non-Niceans (Arians), under the aegis of the heirs of the same Roman emperors who earlier persecuted those who followed the "way" of Christian living, which culminated in the deplorable post-Chalcedonian split that tore apart the body of Christ, and which was recently repeatedly deemed unnecessary by the 20th and 21st century followers of the two camps.[21] So, it is no mere chance that Chrysostom was martyred by Constantinople and Alexandria for preaching the scriptural "word" of instruction and correction.

Epilogue

Just as the Prophets and Paul are alive in that they carried and planted the seed of the divine word, so Chrysostom is still alive in his legacy. What is stunning is the way in which Chrysostom emulated his scriptural teachers not only in their teaching but also, as a true disciple ultimately would, in his end. Actually his end was virtually a copy of the classic scriptural story. Just as with the Prophets, Jesus, and Paul, Chrysostom lived by and for the divine word and he died for it, condemned by a gathering of the religious leaders in collusion with the imperial power! May we be deemed to follow his path in this one world of ours!

· M A R K   D I C K E N S ·

Biblical Fragments from the Christian Library of Turfan, an Eastern Outpost of the Antiochian Tradition

The modern-day city of Turfan (or Turpan), is located at 42°52' N, 89°12' E, approximately 160 km SE of Urumchi, the capital of the Xinjiang Uyghur Autonomous Region in western China, which is in turn bounded to the north by Mongolia, to the south by Tibet and to the west by Kazakhstan and Kyrgyzstan. Situated on the northern perimeter of the Tarim Basin and the Taklamakan Desert, the Turfan Oasis was an important staging post at the junction of two branches of the trade route now called the Silk Road which criss-crossed Central Asia, linking the Chinese Empire to the east and the Persian, Byzantine and later Arab Empires to the west.

As a result, Turfan also played a key role in the political, cultural and religious history of the area, particularly amongst the Turkic peoples. After the rise and fall of the First and Second Türk Empires (552-630, 682-742) in what is now Mongolia, the Turkic Uyghurs established their own Uyghur Empire in 744, also centred in Mongolia. They in turn were toppled by the Kyrgyz in 840 and the Uyghurs scattered, fleeing south to form several smaller states.

One of these states, the Uyghur Kingdom of Qocho, established in the Turfan Oasis ca. 860, lasted more than 400 years, until the Mongols finally absorbed it into their empire in 1284. During those four centuries, Turfan was an extremely important cultural and religious centre in Central Asia. The Uyghurs, who had adopted Manichaeism as their state religion in 763 during the height of their political power, continued to practice that religion in Turfan, although their movement southwards from Mongolia brought them into increasing contact with Buddhism, the dominant religion in Central Asia east of the Tien Shan Mountains at the time. By the Mongol era, the majority of Uyghurs had adopted Buddhism (their eventual conversion to Islam was not completed until the 15th century).

Between 1902 and 1914, four Prussian archaeological expeditions to Turfan brought back a wealth of manuscript fragments and other artefacts to be deposited in Berlin.[1] 40,000 fragments in 20 scripts and 22 languages are now divided between the Berlin-Brandenburg Academy of Sciences, the Oriental Department of the State Library of Berlin and the Museum for Asian Art. Not surprisingly, most manuscript remnants are from Buddhist or Manichaean texts, but a significant minority (somewhat over 1100), brought back by the Second and Third Prussian Turfan Expeditions (1904-1907), are Christian, most of which are written in the Syriac script, dating from the 9th to the 13th/14th century. These fragments are the subject of *The Christian Library at Turfan* Project, funded by the Arts and Humanities Research Council of the United Kingdom and based in the School of Oriental and African Studies (SOAS), University of London.[2]

Christian Manuscripts from Turfan

With the possible exception of a few fragments which may originate in the Melkite (Orthodox) community in Tashkent,[3] the Christian library from Turfan primarily reflects the eastward missionary expansion of the Church of the East (commonly but erroneously referred to as the "Nestorian" Church), which carried the Antiochian exegetical and hermeneutical tradition into Central Asia, China and Mongolia. Although reconstructing the history of this tradition in these areas is particularly difficult, due to the scattered nature of textual and archaeological witnesses, the Christian manuscripts in the Turfan Collection in Berlin shed valuable light on how this stream of Christianity interacted with local languages and cultures.[4]

Indeed, the Turfan corpus constitutes the easternmost extant library of any medieval Christian community, with manuscript fragments in Syriac, Middle Persian, Sogdian, New Persian and Old Turkic. These represent a broad spectrum of genres, including biblical and liturgical texts, ascetic and hagiographical works, and prayer booklets, all indicative of the monastic nature of the community in Bu-layïq in the Turfan Oasis from which they originated.[5] A few Christian manuscript fragments have been recovered from two other sites in western China, Dunhuang (Gansu Province) and Qara-khoto (Inner Mongolia), but they cannot compare in quantity to the sheer volume of the Turfan material.[6] Although many of the Christian texts uncovered at Turfan have been published, a considerable number still require either initial publication or more in-depth scholarly analysis.

Of the 1100+ Christian fragments, slightly more than 450 are Syriac, while approximately 550 are Sogdian in Syriac script, 50 are Sogdian in Sogdian script and 50 are Uyghur (in either Syriac or Uyghur script). In addition, there are a handful of Middle Persian and New Persian Christian fragments. Many of these Christian fragments are in fact bilingual or even multilingual, so that, for example, the total number of fragments wholly or partially in Syriac rises to somewhat over 500. The languages involved reflect the cultural background of not only the Church of the East itself, but also this region of Asia that it had expanded into.

As Nicholas Sims-Williams has pointed out, Syriac was always the primary liturgical language in Bulayïq, but initially Middle Persian and then Sogdian were employed for Bible readings and certain other parts of the liturgy. At some point, Uyghur seems to have eclipsed Sogdian as the primary *lingua franca* in the community. Thus, non-liturgical and non-literary texts were increasingly written in Uyghur, although Sogdian continued to be the most popular language in which ascetical texts were read, judging from the manuscript remains.[7]

Thus, a large portion of the Christian manuscript fragments from Turfan are in **Syriac**, the primary literary and liturgical language of the Church of the East.[8] Most of these are liturgical and biblical fragments, which together probably account for 95% of the Syriac material. A number of other genres are also represented, albeit minimally, including calendrical tables, hagiographies, and prayer booklets or amulets. However, very little of the material has been published in the century since the manuscripts were brought back to Berlin. The exceptions are the following: [9]

1. Several folios from two separate Hudras:[10] **SyrHT 41** (T II B 7 No. 1a)[11] and **MIK III 45** (T II B 26);[12]
2. Part of the Legend of Mar Barshabba, the legendary founder of the church in Merv: **SyrHT 45 & 46** (T II B 9 No. 3);[13]

3. A pharmaceutical recipe: **SyrHT 1** (T II B 17 No. 4);[14]
4. A letter, seemingly to a Byzantine official: **SyrHT 2** (T II B 18 No. 1b and T II B 62 No. 1a);[15]
5. Fragments of a previously unknown version of the Legend of St. George: **SyrHT 95, 359-362, 364-365** (T II B 31, No. 2 & 3, T II B 51, T II B 53 and T II B 66 No. 45);[16]
6. A dialogue between a Jew and a Christian: **SyrHT 94** (T II B 50).[17]

Sogdian was an Eastern Middle Iranian language spoken in Sogdiana (modern-day Uzbekistan and Tajikistan), as well as in the Sogdian *Diaspora* that stretched eastward into China (the Sogdians were inveterate traders and controlled much of the commerce on the middle portion of the Silk Road). The corpus of Sogdian Christian material from Turfan, written in both Syriac and Sogdian scripts, encompasses biblical, liturgical, ascetical, hagiographical and secular texts and has been described several times.[18] Many individual works have been published, including the following (excluding biblical texts, which are addressed below):[19]

1. A Sogdian version of the Legend of St. George: **n1-n11** and other fragments (T II B 30, T II B 66, T II B 67);[20]
2. A large manuscript, labelled C2, containing hagiographical, homiletic and ascetical texts;[21]
3. Part of a "Book of Life," commemorating the dead: **n396** (T II B 40);[22]
4. A collection of riddles on biblical subjects: **n349-n353** (T II B 22, T II B 57);[23]
5. A translation of the hymn "Gloria in excelsis Deo": **n192** (T II B 66, T III B);[24]
6. A history of Mar Serapion: **n284** and other lost fragments (T III B);[25]
7. A history of Mar Awgen: **n443, n167, n426, n235, n368, n169** (T II B 60, T II B 65, T II B 66);[26]
8. A Christian polemic against the Manichaeans: **n145** (T II B 8).[27]

Middle Persian, the language of Sassanid Persia, was gradually replaced by **New Persian** in the centuries following the Arab conquest of Iran and Central Asia. Although these languages were primarily used to the west of the Tien Shan Mountains (in Iran proper and the Iranian-speaking areas of Central Asia), the Turfan documents suggest that both also had a limited presence in Chinese Central Asia. The only Christian text in Middle Persian is the so-called Pahlavi Psalter, described below. New Persian texts in Syriac script are limited to one and a half folios from a bilingual Syriac-New Persian Psalter, also described below, and two remnants of a pharmacological text: **M 7340** (T II Toyoq) and **n175** (T II B 69 + T II B 14).

There are also a limited number of Christian texts in **Old Uyghur**, one of several Turkic languages that evolved out of Old Turkic (indeed, Old Uyghur can be considered a dialect of Old Turkic). These texts are written in both Syriac and Uyghur script and have been described on several occasions.[28] Important texts that have been published so far include:

1. A unique Central Asian version of the Legend of the Magi: *U **9175** (T II B 29);[29]
2. An oracle book or collection of apocryphal sayings, including a non-canonical quotation from Luke: **U 320** (T II B 1);[30]
3. A passage from the Legend of St. George: **MIK III 194** (T II B 66);[31]
4. A wedding blessing: **U 7264** (T III Kurutka);[32]
5. A fragment from a Creed: **U 5537 & U 5538** (T II B 17);[33]
6. A prayer booklet with passages in both Syriac and Uyghur: **U 338** (T II B 41).[34]

Christian Manuscripts from Turfan

Based on the evidence of the extant Christian texts from Turfan, including orthographic errors in many of the Syriac language fragments, it is clear that the Turfan Christians were predominantly Sogdian and Uyghur speakers,[35] although the presence of a few Persian texts suggests that that language may also have been spoken by some in the community. Whether or not there were any native Syriac speakers at any time in Turfan is unclear. Given the extensive ecclesiastical network throughout Central Asia,[36] it is not unlikely that those who initially carried Christianity to Turfan were from Central Asia themselves, although we can only speculate about their ethnicity.[37]

However, despite the eastward direction of the Church's mission, the Turfan documents clearly show a westward orientation in terms of theological influence. Whether the Peshitta version of the Bible, the standard liturgical texts of the Church of the East, the hagiographical materials translated into Sogdian or the prayer booklets containing amuletic material, the vast majority of the Turfan Christian texts have clear antecedents in the Middle Eastern heartland of the Church. It is only when we come to the Uyghur Christian materials that we start to encounter some indications of influence from the multi-religious environment at Turfan, such as the use of the Buddhist concept of merit transfer by the Uyghur scribe who wrote the prayer booklet **U 338**.[38] Nevertheless, other than a few texts like this, there is no widespread evidence of syncretism and certainly none of the "heresy" which the mislabelled "Nestorian" Church is so often accused of.[39]

Perhaps the clearest indication of the "orthodoxy" of the Turfan Christians can be found in **MIK III 59** (T II B 17 + T II B 28), a Sogdian version of the Nicene Creed found at Turfan:

> We believe in one God, the Father, who upholds everything, the Creator of all things that are seen and unseen. [We believe] in one Lord God, and in Jesus [Christ], the only son of God, [the firstborn] of all beings, who... in the beginning was not created but begotten by the Father, [true God] of the true God... by whose hand the [aeons] were fashioned and everything was created, he who for the sake of men and for our salvation descended from the heavens and clothed himself in a body by the Holy Spirit, and became man and entered the womb; who was born of Mary, the virgin, and [who] suffered agony and [was] raised on the cross [in] the days of Pontius Pilate; and [was buried] and ascended and sits on the right hand of the Father and is ready to come (again) to judge the dead and the living. And [we believe] in the Spirit of Truth, the Holy Spirit, who went forth from the Father, the Holy Spirit who gives life, and in one Holy Apostolic Christian Church.[40]

As the above creed indicates, and given the theological roots of the Church of the East, there is an understandably strong Antiochian component within this overall orientation back to the Middle Eastern homeland of Christianity. This includes an acknowledgement of the theological debt to both the Greek Doctors and the Syrian Doctors in the Antiochian tradition. Thus, we find in **SyrHT 80** (T II B 42 No. 1a, part of an original manuscript currently designated as Hudra "F") the following passage from the Martyrs' Anthems (ܥܘܢܝܬܐ ܕܣܗܕܐ, *'onyāthā d-sahdē*) for the Friday before the Rogation of the Ninevites (a three-day fast in the tenth week before Easter) which celebrates the Doctors of the School of Nisibis, the flagship theological school of the Church of the East:

ܩܠ ܐܠܗܐ ܕܢܣܝܒܝܢ ܒܬܪܝܗܘܢ ܐܬܘܬܐ ܥܠ [41]ܥܠ ܫܘܒܚܐ
ܥܡ ܪܒܢ ܬܐܘܕܘܪܐ ܘܕܝܘܕܘܪܐ ܥܡ ܦܪܨܘܦܐܗܘ ܦܪܨܘܦܐܢ ܐܒܗܝ

ܐܬܝܢ ܠܟܝܢܬܐ ܘܪܒܐܢ ܝܘܚܢܢ ܥܡ ⁴²ܐܒܪܗܡ, ܘܢܪܣܝ, ܝܘܐ, ܝܕܒ
⁴³.ܘܡܝܟܐܝܠ

He set upon.[44] Upon the foundation of the truth of Simon Peter (Cephas) built the orthodox Diodore and Theodore with Nestorius, and the Great Ephrem with Mar Narsai and Mar Abraham with John, Job and Michael, the heirs of truth.[45]

This text (along with others in the East Syriac liturgy) shows the unapologetic appreciation of the Church of the East for Diodore of Tarsus, Theodore of Mopsuestia and Nestorius himself, although it should be noted that the Church has never referred to itself as "Nestorian." That term has only been used by its theological opponents or those of other faiths, such as the Muslims, for whom the Christological disputes of the 4th century were irrelevant.[46]

In this anthem, the three Greek Doctors of the Antiochian tradition are followed by important Syrian Doctors connected with Nisibis. Ephrem the Syrian (d. 373) taught at the School of Nisibis before the Persians captured the city in 363, forcing the school to relocate to Edessa. After the School of Edessa was closed by Emperor Zeno in 489 because of its "Nestorian" tendencies, forcing scholars to flee to Nisibis in Persian territory, Mar Narsai re-founded the School there. Abraham of Beth Rabban was the third head of the School in Nisibis (after Elisha bar Quzbaye) and was in turn succeeded by John of Beth Rabban in the mid-6th century. Job the Persian translated various theological works into Persian in the 6th century and Michael Badoqa (the Expositor) was a student of Hannana of Adiabene, head of the School in the late 6th century.[47]

Another indication of the Antiochian theological perspective can be found in **SyrHT 279-284** (T II S 25 No. 1), several folios from a small booklet containing a prayer to the Virgin Mary which refers to her frequently as ܒܬܘܠܬܐ ܩܕܝܫܬܐ ܐܡܗ ܕܡܫܝܚܐ (*btholtā qdhishtā ameh d-mashi+ā*), "the Holy Virgin, Mother of Christ," the Syriac equivalent of *Christotokos*.[48] Not surprisingly, the term ܐܡܗ ܕܐܠܗܐ (*ameh d-alāhā*), "Mother of God," equivalent to *Theotokos*, is nowhere to be found in the Turfan materials.

However, those in the Alexandrian tradition are not entirely neglected, as the Desert Fathers, including a number of Coptic saints, are mentioned with reverence in the East Syriac liturgy, not to mention the frequent references to them amongst the aforementioned hagiographical and ascetical works translated into Sogdian. One such Syriac reference can be found in **SyrHT 178** (T II B 66 No. 22, part of an original manuscript designated as Hudra "D"):

ܚܘ ܠܥ ܐܝܪܐ ܐܝܪܣܡܗܪ ܢܝܫܝܪܐ ܩܠܐܘ ܐܝܪܓܠܘܐܘ
ܘܢܡܝܗܩܘ ܪܐ ܐܝܪܘܡܐܘ ܐܝܪܐ ܓܝܫܝܐ ܐܝܪܐ ܠܥ
ܘܢܡܝܩܘ ܐܝܩܐܘܐܘ ܓܝ ܐܣܘܡܚܘ ܐܝܝܪܐ ܐܝܩܝܝܪ܀

The solitary fathers (i.e. anchorites) lived on the earth: Paul, Anthony and Macarius, also Arsenius, Evagrius, Awgen, Isaiah, Mark and Amun with Pachomius and the rest of the holy ones.[49]

The ascetics mentioned here are St. Paul the Anchorite (d. ca. 341), St. Anthony the Great (d. 356), St. Macarius of Egypt (d. 391), St. Arsenius of Scete (d. 445), Evagrius Ponticus (d. 399), Mar Awgen (Eugenius), the founder of coenobitic monasticism in Mesopotamia (d. ca. 379), Abba Isaiah of Scete (late 4th cent.), Mark the Monk (5th cent.), St. Amun of the Nitrian Desert (d. 357), and St. Pachomius, the founder of coenobitic monasticism in Egypt (d. 348).[50]

Biblical Fragments from Turfan

The importance of the biblical text in a monastic community that was continually celebrating the liturgy needs no explanation. Thus it is no surprise to find a significant number of biblical fragments from Turfan. However, due to their fragmentary nature and later dating (9th-13th/14th centuries), they are neither the most complete nor the earliest manuscripts of the Peshitta text and so are of less value in tracking variations in the text.[51] With one exception, biblical texts from Turfan can be divided into Psalter fragments, Gospel fragments and lectionary fragments. Having described the Turfan Psalter texts in-depth elsewhere,[52] after a brief summary of them here, I will focus on the non-Psalter texts.

Whereas the West Syriac (Syrian Orthodox and Maronite) tradition has used several different translations of the Bible, including the Syrohexaplar version of the Old Testament and the Philoxenian and Harklean versions of the New Testament,[53] the only Bible translation consistently used in the East Syriac tradition is the Peshitta and this is clearly seen in the biblical fragments from Turfan. Not surprisingly, the composition and organisation of the Peshitta differs somewhat from other translations.

Manuscripts of the Peshitta Old Testament usually include the Deuterocanonical (Apocryphal) books, although some contain additional books such as 3 and 4 Maccabees, 4 Ezra or the Apocalypse of Baruch.[54] Occasionally additional Psalms (Ps. 151-155) are included.[55] Thus far, neither the Deuterocanonical books nor the extra Psalms have been found amongst the Turfan fragments. The numbering of the Psalms also differs from that of both the Masoretic text (hereafter MT) and the Septuagint (hereafter LXX). Ps. 114 and 115 in the MT are combined into Ps. 114 in the Peshitta, leaving the Peshitta Psalm numbers one behind the Hebrew numbers up to Ps. 147 in the MT, which is divided into Ps. 146 and 147 in the Peshitta; thus, the last three Psalm numbers are the same in both traditions.[56] Psalm numbers in Syriac Psalters are either spelled out or given with letters from the Syriac alphabet, each of which has a numerical equivalent.[57]

The Psalter in the East Syriac tradition (including the Odes, described below) consists of 21 major divisions called ܚܘܼܠܵܐ (sg. *hulālā*, pl. *hulālē*). Each *hulālā* is further divided into several smaller sections called ܡܲܪܡܝܵܬ݂ܵܐ (sg. *marmithā*, pl. *marmayāthā*), each of which contains several Psalms. Most East Syriac Psalters also include the following additional components:

1. Headings or titles: derived from the commentaries of Theodore of Mopsuestia on the Psalms (and therefore different from the headings in the MT or LXX), these occur after the Psalm numbers, usually in rubric.

2. Prayers: relating to the subject of the next Psalm or group of Psalms, these are inserted at the beginning of each new *hulālā* or *marmithā*, after the heading and the word ܨܠܘܿܬ݂ܐ (*ṣlothā*), "prayer," in rubric; the prayers themselves are in black ink.

3. Farcings or canons: relating to the subject of each Psalm and attributed to Patriarch Mar Aba I (540-552), these short sentences are inserted after the first verse or between the first and second half of the first verse, usually in rubric.

4. Odes or canticles: the following Psalm-like passages from elsewhere in the Old Testament are included at the end of most East Syriac Psalters: Exod. 15:1-21 (the First Song of Moses); Deut. 32:1-43 (the Second and Third Songs of Moses); Isa. 42:10-13; 45:8 (the Song of Isaiah).

Syriac Psalters

We are fortunate to have fragments from a wide range of Psalters amongst the Turfan materials, both in Syriac and in other languages.[58] Thus far, remnants of 11 Syriac Psalters have been identified. Following the lead of the anonymous compiler of a typed hand-list of the Syriac fragments in the Turfan Collection, who identified some of the fragments from Psalter "C," Psalter "D" and Psalter "E," the original manuscripts have been identified as Psalters "C" through "M."[59] The Psalters can be summarized as follows (individual fragment signature numbers and contents are given in Appendix I):

1. **Psalter "C"**: nine folios stitched together in booklet form plus four separate fragments, with headings, canons, prayers, quire marks and indication of new *marmayāthā*.
2. **Psalter "D"**: 12 fragments in a very distinctive hand, with headings and canons (but no prayers), quire marks, Psalm numbers and indication of new *marmayāthā*.
3. **Psalter "E"**: four adjacent folios stitched together in booklet form plus a small fragment that can be joined to one of the folios, with headings, canons, prayers, Psalm numbers and a distinctive mark in the upper right verso corner of each folio.
4. **Psalter "F"**: 15 fragments in another distinctive hand with each line consisting of exactly one colon of the biblical text (sometimes necessitating the omission of extraneous words at the end of each line), canons and prayers, but no headings.
5. **Psalter "G"**: one folio in yet another distinctive hand, again consisting of exactly one colon of the text per line, resulting in omitted words at the end of most lines, but without headings, canons or prayers.
6. **Psalter "H"**: one folio with only one colon per line, all lines ending in ❖ and many lines ending with ܗܘܠܠܐ (*Hallelujah*) as a space-filler.Odes or canticles: the following Psalm-like passages from elsewhere in the Old Testament are included at the end of most East Syriac Psalters: Exod. 15:1-21 (the First Song of Moses); Deut. 32:1-43 (the Second and Third Songs of Moses); Isa. 42:10-13; 45:8 (the Song of Isaiah).
7. **Psalter "I"**: one folio with only one colon per line, all lines ending in ❖ and many lines ending with ܗܘܠܠܐ, with canons and prayers, but no headings.

8. **Psalter "J"**: two fragments, including a double-folio, with only one colon per line and all lines ending in ❖, resulting again in omitted words, with canons and prayers, but no headings.
9. **Psalter "K"**: five fragments with headings and a cross visible in the upper right corner of one folio, but no canons or prayers.
10. **Psalter "L"**: two fragments from the same original folio.
11. **Psalter "M"**: one small fragment in an attractive hand.[60]
12. **Psalter "N"**: eight fragments, with headings, but no canons or prayers.
13. **Psalter "O"**: six fragments, with headings, but no canons or prayers.
14. **Psalter "P"**: part of one folio, arranged in two columns and, like Psalter "G," without headings, canons or prayers and with words missing at the end of each line.
15. **Psalter "Q"**: one fragment, with headings, but no canons or prayers.

Another distinctive Psalter from Turfan consists of nine folios from a small booklet, written in Syriac transliterated into Uyghur script: **SyrHT 20-27** and **MIK III 58** (T II B 10). Obviously prepared to help Uyghur-speaking monks to recite the Syriac liturgy, it includes, in addition to six folios containing Psalms, three folios with hymns by Syriac authors (such as Ephrem the Syrian) known as ܬܫܒܘܚܬܐ (sg. *teshbo✝tā*, pl. *teshb✝āthā*), also used extensively in the liturgy.[61]

Finally, there are also excerpts from the Psalms in texts that are clearly not Psalters. One such text is **SyrHT 386** (T II D20i 5+6). Ps. 148:1-3 is written in reverse order in a rough hand on one side, while on the reverse side someone has drawn a circular doodle around a hole in the paper, embellished with what looks like hair and ears, similar in appearance to illustrations of Uyghurs on other fragments in the Turfan Collection.[62] The biblical text is as follows:

ܫܒܚܘ 1
ܫܒܚܘܗܝ, ܫܡܫܐ ܘܣܗܪܐ 2
ܗܒ ,ܫܒܚܘܗܝ❖[63], 3
ܫܒܚܘܗܝ, ܠܟܠܗܘܢ ܡ'ܠܐ 4
ܫܒܚܘܗܝ, ܒܡܪ̈ܘܡܐ 5
ܫܒܚܘ ܠܡܪܝܐ ܡܢ ܫܡܝܐ 6

1. Praise...
2. Praise him, sun and moon
3. -els.[64] Praise him
4. Praise him, all his ang-
5. Praise him in the heights

6. Praise the Lord from the heavens.

Non-Syriac Psalters

In addition to the Syriac Psalters, the following Psalters in other languages have also been identified:

1. **Pahlavi Psalter**: 12 folios[65] written in Pahlavi script, containing portions of Ps. 94-99, 118 (= MT Ps. 119) and 121-136 (= MT Ps. 122-137) and generally translated from the Peshitta, although showing the influence of the MT or LXX in places.[66]

2. **Sogdian Psalter 1**: 15 fragments[67] written in Sogdian script (including the Sogdian version of the Nicene Creed mentioned above), containing portions of Ps. 5-6, 19-20, 23-24, 28-30, 32, 33, 50, and 51, translated from the Peshitta with the first verse of each Psalm in both Syriac and Sogdian.[68]

3. **Sogdian Psalter 2**: 2 fragments[69] written in Sogdian script, containing Ps. 33:1-4, 8-10 and Ps. 34:7-9, 14-16, which follow the Peshitta in places and the LXX in others, with the opening words of each Psalm in a Greek headline in the upper margin.[70]

4. **Syriac-New Persian Psalter**: 2 fragments[71] written in Syriac script, containing Ps. 131:18-132:1; 133:1-3; 146:5-147:7 (= MT Ps. 132:18-133:1; 134:1-3; 147:5-18), translated from the Peshitta with each colon of the text given in Syriac, followed by New Persian.[72]

Apart from the Psalter remnants, there is only one other Turfan fragment containing an Old Testament text, the exception noted above. On the back side of T II B 18 No. 1b, one of the two fragments that make up **SyrHT 2**, the Syriac letter mentioned above, is the Peshitta text of Proverbs 9:14-10:12, written in black ink in a hand similar (or perhaps identical) to that in which the letter is written in brown ink.

The different texts on the reverse side of the two fragments suggest that they were miscellaneous scraps of paper that the scribe used for writing his letter (which is likely a template or draft version). Thus, the Proverbs text probably pre-exists the letter, but it is impossible to speculate further without other folios or fragments from the original biblical manuscript.[73] If indeed the letter originated in the Melkite community in Tashkent, this might explain why it is the only non-Psalter text from the Old Testament found in Turfan. It is also impossible to tell if the text was originally part of an Old Testament manuscript or an Old Testament lectionary. Although the calendars of East

Syriac lectionary readings published by Maclean and Diettrich (based on later manuscripts and printed books) do not include Proverbs, the 6th century Syriac lectionary published by Burkitt (BL Add. 14528) gives Proverbs 9:1-10:26 as the reading for Easter Day.[74]

Syriac New Testament Fragments

The canon of the Peshitta New Testament differs from that of the Catholic and Orthodox traditions, in that the books of 2 Peter, 2 John, 3 John, Jude and Revelation are not included.[75] In addition, the General Epistles follow the Gospels and Acts and are in turn followed by the Pauline Epistles, ending with the Epistle to the Hebrews. The New Testament books are divided up into sections, each called a ܨܚܚܐ (sg. *܀+ā+ā*, pl. *܀+ā+ē*), which are somewhat longer than the chapters in the division of the text used in the West. Thus, in Matthew, ܨܚܚܐ ܐ (section 1) begins at 1:1, ܨܚܚܐ ܒ (section 2) begins at 2:19, ܨܚܚܐ ܓ (section 3) begins at 5:1 and so on. Although section numbering begins again at ܐ for each of the Gospels, Acts is grouped together with the General Epistles and the Pauline Epistles are also grouped together.[76] These sections are used to designate readings in Syriac lectionaries.

Since the biblical fragments from Turfan containing New Testament passages are rarely more than one or at the most two folios and often little more than a fragment, it is sometimes difficult to determine whether or not a fragment containing a New Testament text is from a lectionary or not. Thankfully, some fragments include the lectionary headings in rubric, but others give no clue, due to the minimal text they contain. The lectionary fragments come from either gospel lectionaries or Pauline epistle lectionaries; no texts from either Acts or the General Epistles have been discovered so far.[77] Following the system of identifying the Syriac Psalters, the Syriac Lectionaries are designated "A," "B" and possibly "C."[78]

Lectionary "A" (which appears to be in the same hand as Lectionary "B," Psalter "C" and Psalter "K") was presumably a lectionary of Pauline epistles, based on the extant fragments::

1. **SyrHT 48 & 49** (T II B 11 No. 11) is a double folio containing the following readings:

a. Romans 1:24-25, end of the reading for the First Monday in Lent;
b. Romans 1:26-2:6, reading for the First Tuesday in Lent;
c. heading for the reading for the First Wednesday in Lent;
d. Romans 5:12-21, end of the reading for the Second Sunday in Lent;
e. Romans 7:1-7, beginning of the reading for the Second Friday in Lent.[79]

2. **SyrHT 373** (T II B 53 No. 8) is a small fragment containing the following readings:
a. Romans 15:9-11, from the reading for the Sixth Friday of Lent;
b. Romans 11:17-18, from the reading for Palm Sunday.[80]

3. **SyrHT 380** (T II B 53 No. 8) is another small fragment containing the following reading:
a. Romans 12:13-16, from the reading for either Tuesday in the Rogation of the Ninevites or the Fifth Sunday in Lent;
b. 1 Corinthians 12:19-20, from the reading for Pentecost.[81]

4. **n438** (T II B 60) is an unidentified small fragment.

5. **SyrHT 370** (T II B 53 No. 8) is another unidentified small fragment.

Lectionary "A" has two interesting features. The first it shares with Lectionary "B" and the bilingual lectionaries described below, namely the use of accents to aid the reader in chanting the biblical text, appearing as large dots above or below each line, quite distinct from vocalization and other diacritic marks.[82]

The other feature of interest on **SyrHT 48 & 49** is the following marginal note in Sogdian script located on the lower margin of one folio, which has been read by Nicholas Sims-Williams as *'yny pwsty ...* "This book ..." Since it is located on the last side of the double folio, it presumably continued onto a now lost folio, perhaps continuing "belongs to N."

Lectionary "B" is represented thus far by only one folio, reconstructed from four separate fragments – **SyrHT 241** (T II B 67b), **SyrHT 277** (T II D 114), **SyrHT 300** (T III B) and **n327** (T II B 66) – which together contain Luke 1:1-21, from the reading for the First Sunday of Advent, a reading also found in **n212**, the only representative of E4, a Syriac-Sogdian gospel lectionary discussed below.[83] This reconstructed folio is a typical challenge for those attempting to decipher the Turfan materials, so many of which have been torn to pieces, apparently deliberately.

There are three Syriac fragments which are probably from original gospel manuscripts rather than gospel lectionaries:

6. **Gospel "A": SyrHT 123** (T II B 58 No. 1b), containing John 3:21-36 – since ⟍ in the margin clearly marks the beginning of a new section of the biblical text at 3:22 and what would be a new reading in the lectionary (but without any rubric indicating this), it is almost certainly not from a lectionary.[84]

7. **Gospel "B": SyrHT 324 & 325** (T III T 297), containing Matthew 16:5-6; 17:1-3 – the first reading is not included in the lectionaries as published by Maclean, Diettrich and Burkitt.[85]

8. **Gospel "C": SyrHT 326** (1858), containing Mark 6:27-33, 36-41 – since the reading for the Feast of St. John the Baptist is only Mark 6:14-30, this cannot be from a lectionary.[86] Like many of the Turfan fragments, there are scribal errors, including two cases of haplography.

It is unclear whether **SyrHT 383** (T II B 53), containing John 7:4-6, 8-10 is from a lectionary (in which case, **Lectionary "C"**) or a Gospel (in which case **Gospel "D"**). If it is from a lectionary, the reading is from the Fourth Thursday in Lent.[87]

Syriac Sogdian New Testament Fragments

Amongst the Christian Sogdian materials in Syriac script, remnants of the following five lectionaries and a sixth text (which is from either a gospel lectionary or a gospel manuscript) have been identified (individual fragment signature numbers and contents are given in Appendix II):[88]

1. **E1**: a Syriac-Sogdian gospel or possibly gospel lectionary (three fragments);
2. **E2**: a Syriac-Sogdian gospel lectionary (three fragments);
3. **E3**: another Syriac-Sogdian gospel lectionary (one fragment);
4. **E4**: another Syriac-Sogdian gospel lectionary (one fragment);
5. **E5**: a Sogdian gospel lectionary with Syriac rubrics indicating the lections (multiple fragments);
6. **E6**: a Syriac-Sogdian Pauline epistle lectionary (ten fragments).

Thus we have four or possibly five Sogdian gospel lectionaries and one lectionary of Pauline epistles. As noted above, these lectionaries all have the recitation accents used to assist in cantillation of the texts. In addition, **n222** (C45), a long narrow strip of uncertain contents, with only 1-2 characters visible on each line, may represent yet another bilingual lectionary fragment. As Nicholas Sims-Williams has observed, certain final letters suggest Sogdian words, whereas other letters and diacritic points suggest Syriac words. Dots that appear to be recitation accents would also suggest that this fragment comes from a lectionary, although any further identification is highly unlikely.[89]

In addition to the recitation accents, another interesting aspect of these lectionaries is the fact that some fragments include readings not contained in the lectionaries published by Maclean, Diettrich and Burkitt. This presumably reflects the fact that the Turfan lectionaries are somewhat later in date than those consulted by Burkitt (most of which are 6th/7th century), but significantly earlier than those consulted by Diettrich (who used a 17th century manuscript) and Maclean (who used a lectionary printed by the Archbishop of Canterbury's Mission at Urmia in 1889). Thus, the texts from Turfan reflect a stage in the development of the text midway between "the earliest liturgical monument of Syriac Christianity that is preserved in approximate completeness" and the current fixed form of the lectionary.[90]

Elsewhere, Burkitt noted a number of Turfan lectionary readings that are not found in either BL Add. 14528 or Cambridge UL Add. 1975, a 16th century lectionary he used as a separate reference,[91] including:

1. Luke 16:2-15 (**n153** = T II B 12);[92]
2. Luke 19:15-27 (*T II B 39);[93]
3. Matthew 25:31-46 (**n164** = T II B 66; *T II B 39), the reading for the commemoration of Mar Barshabba according to the rubric;[94]
4. Matthew 16:24-17:7 (**n164** = T II B 66, T II B 17 and T II B 62), the reading for the commemoration of Mar Sergius and Mar Bacchus;[95]
5. Luke 13:3-4 (**n152** = T II B 66);[96]
6. Luke 12:35-39, 42-44 (**n165** = T III B 52 and **n413c** = T III B);[97]
7. John 5:19 (**n165** = T III B 52).[98]

Perhaps most noteworthy is the inclusion of a lectionary reading for Mar Barshabba, traditionally commemorated as the one who brought Christianity to Merv, the jumping off point for subsequent missions of the Church of the East into Central Asia and other points to the north and east. The fact that he is not included in extant East Syriac lectionaries from the Middle East presumably reflects the limitation of his "sphere of influence" to just Central Asia.[99]

New Testament verses or passages also occur in Turfan texts that are neither gospels nor lectionaries. One such example is a prayer amulet, composed of two fragments: **SyrHT 99** (T II B 53 = 1687) and **SyrHT 330** (1863), which begins with a quotation from John 1:1-5, "In the beginning was the Word, and the Word was with God, and the Word was God..." a typical opening statement on Syriac prayer amulets intended to impress both the wearer and any malevolent beings intent on bringing harm with the power of the word of God and hence the efficacy of the amulet written to protect the wearer from harm.[100] Another example is ܒܝܪܚܐ ܫܬܝܬܝܐ ܐܫܬܠܚ ܓܒܪܝܠ, "In the sixth month, Gabriel was sent..." the beginning of Luke 1:26, written on the reverse of T II B 62 No. 1a, one of the two fragments making up **SyrHT 2**, the aforementioned letter. Written in a different hand from that of the letter, its appearance as marginalia prompts one to wonder if the writer was listening to a sermon during the Advent season while he penned this line on a back of scrap paper, later to be re-used by the author of the letter.

Conclusion

The Christian manuscript fragments from Turfan are a rich treasure trove of information on how a community in the Antiochian theological tradition conducted itself far from the original homeland of that tradition. The fragments in Syriac, Sogdian and Uyghur shed light on how the Turfan Christians both maintained ties with their theological roots and related to the surrounding culture. The texts reveal a westward theological orientation in the context of the overall eastward direction of the Church's mission to Central Asia and China. Although evidence of interaction with the surrounding Buddhist and Manichaean milieu can be detected, the documents do not give evidence of widespread syncretism in the Christian community. Indeed, the texts are largely what one would expect to find in a monastic community in the Church of the East.

Amongst the Christian texts are a significant number of biblical fragments, mostly from Psalters and lectionaries. They affirm the central role that the Bible has always played in the liturgy of the Church of the East, particularly in monastic communities. The presence of Psalter texts in not only Syriac, but also Middle Persian, Sogdian and New Persian, as well as extracts from the Psalms in Syriac in Uyghur script, testifies to the importance of hearing and understanding the biblical text in both the liturgical language of the Church and the various languages spoken throughout Central Asia during the medieval period. The same can be said of the lectionaries containing New Testament material, extant in both Syriac and Sogdian. Unfortunately, the fragmentary nature of the Christian texts from Turfan makes it difficult to speculate much on why certain texts, especially non-Psalter books of the Old Testament, are not found amongst the biblical fragments. Other questions hinted at in the biblical fragments, such as possible relationships between the Turfan Christians and the Central Asian Melkites, also remain unanswered for the time being.

Certainly, there is still considerable scope for scholars to analyze the Christian texts from Turfan, including the biblical fragments. Scribal errors could potentially reveal how the Syriac texts were pronounced by native speakers of Sogdian and Uyghur. Comparison of the Syriac lectionary texts (particularly the recitation accents) with contemporary examples found in the Middle East may shed more light on how these texts were chanted in the liturgy at this time. Perhaps too, a study of the jottings and graffiti written on the Christian fragments, whether biblical or otherwise, would reveal something of how those in the monastic community interacted with the text. Although the remnants are relatively few in number, they can also help to fill out our knowledge of the evolution of the lectionary system in the Church of the East, including local variants found in Central Asia. Finally, biblical quotations or allusions in non-liturgical texts, such as prayer amulets, remind us that the biblical text was also used outside of the liturgy, in the context of day-to-day life.

Appendix I: Syriac Psalter Signature Numbers[101]

Psalter "C"

- **SyrHT 72, ff. 1-2 & SyrHT 348** = Ps. 72:18-74:1
- **SyrHT 72, f. 3** = Ps. 117:23-118:4 (= MT Ps. 118:23-119:4)

- **SyrHT 228** & **SyrHT 379** = Ps. 137:7-138 title, 2-8 (= MT Ps. 138:7-139 title, 2-8)
- **SyrHT 79** = Ps. 140:1-141:2 (= MT Ps. 141:1-142:2)
- **SyrHT 72, ff. 4-5** = Ps. 143:5-144:17 (= MT Ps. 144:5-145:17)
- **SyrHT 72, ff. 6-9** = Ps. 145:9-150:4 (= MT Ps. 146:9-150:4)

Psalter "D"

- **SyrHT 129** = Ps. 72:8-73:4
- **SyrHT 377** = Ps. 74:21-23; 75:8-10
- **SyrHT 180** = Ps. 87:1-88:12
- **SyrHT 119** = Ps. 89:12-20, 23-33
- **SyrHT 224 (I)** = Ps. 89:35-42, 48-53; 95:4-7; 96:1-2
- **SyrHT 64** = Ps. 89:46-47; 90:2
- **SyrHT 157** = Ps. 92:8-13; 93:1-5
- **SyrHT 239** = Ps. 94:12-15, 23-95:1
- **SyrHT 224 (II)** = Ps. 95:4-7; 96:1-2
- **SyrHT 63** = Ps. 95:9-10; 96:5-8
- **SyrHT 308** = Ps. 103:2-4, 14-16
- **SyrHT 191** = Ps. 118:133-142, 146-153 (= MT Ps. 119:133-142, 146-153)

Psalter "E"

- **SyrHT 71** = Ps. 22:8-26:3

Psalter "F"

- **SyrHT 14, 15 & 17** = Ps. 66:13-15; 67:5-6
- **SyrHT 174** = Ps. 73:25-27; 74:4-7
- **SyrHT 90** = Ps. 78:26-45
- **SyrHT 91** = 78:46-64
- **SyrHT 93** = 79:9-80:12
- **SyrHT 92** = Ps. 84:3-85:5
- **SyrHT 172, SyrHT 175 & n418** = Ps. 85:6-12; 86:1-8
- **SyrHT 173, SyrHT 176 & SyrHT 177** = Ps. 90:2-7, 9-16
- **SyrHT 367** = currently unidentifiable

Psalter "G"

- **SyrHT 96** = Exod. 15:15-21; Isa. 42:10-13; 45:8

Psalter "H"

- **SyrHT 62** = Deut. 32:31-40

Psalter "I"

- **SyrHT 108** = Ps. 10:12-12:3

Psalter "J"

- **SyrHT 113** = Ps. 14:7-16:5; 18:35-50
- **SyrHT 164** = Ps. 18:51-19:2; 19:4-7

Psalter "K"

- **SyrHT 120** = Ps. 35:7-17, 22-36:3
- **SyrHT 121** = Ps. 36:7-37:2, 7-16
- **SyrHT 220** = Ps. 37:20-23, 34-38
- **SyrHT 357** = Ps. 38:9-12; 39:2-3
- **SyrHT 358** = Ps. 141:5-8 (= MT Ps. 142:5-8); 143:15-144:4 (= MT Ps. 144:15-145:4)

Psalter "L"

- **SyrHT 98** & **SyrHT 203** = Ps. 118:32-49, 63-80 (= MT Ps. 119:32-49, 63-80)

Psalter "M"

- **MIK III 110** = Ps. 24:3-4; 25:3-6

Psalter "N"

- **SyrHT 382** = Ps. 22:26-30; 23:6-24:4
- **SyrHT 4-7 + SyrHT 295** = Ps. 65:8-66:4; 66:7-67 heading
- **n301** = Ps. 83:8-14; 84:3-8
- **SyrHT 181** = Ps. 84:10-85:3; 85:12-86:5

Psalter "O"

- **SyrHT 313** = Ps. 22:21-24, 27-29
- **SyrHT 312** = Ps. 23:1-3, 23:6-24:2
- **SyrHT 314** = Ps. 24:7-9; 25:2-5
- **SyrHT 333** & **SyrHT 315** = Ps. 25:10-12, 18-21
- **SyrHT 378** = Ps. 101:2-3; 102:1

Psalter "P"

- **SyrHT 230** = Ps. 9:20-10:14; 10:17-11:1

Psalter "Q"

- **SyrHT 342** = Ps. 2:7-11; 3:9-4:4

Uyghur Psalter

- **SyrHT 23** = Ps. 11:6-13:3
- **SyrHT 26** = Ps. 13:3-14:7
- **SyrHT 20** = Ps. 14:7; 99:1-100:1
- **SyrHT 22** = Ps. 101:1-8
- **MIK III 58** = Ps. 86:11-87:7
- **SyrHT 21** = Ps. 87:7-88:15

Appendix I: Syriac-Sodgian Psalter Lectionary Signature Numbers[102]

E1 = Syriac-Sogdian gospel or possibly gospel lectionary[103]

- **n177** = Matthew 1:5-7
- **n178** = Matthew 1:10-13
- **n213** = Matthew 6:20-23, 29-32

E2 = Syriac-Sogdian gospel lectionary

- **n214**= John 14:28-30; 16:4-7
- **n223 & n224** = Matthew 19:10-11, 17-18

E3 = Syriac-Sogdian gospel lectionary

- **n190** = Luke 2:10-20; Matthew 2:1-3

E4 = Syriac-Sogdian gospel lectionary

- **n212** = Luke 1:1-4

E5 = Sogdian gospel lectionary with Syriac rubrics[104]

- **n166** = Luke 1:44, 55-56
- **n149** = John 1:19-28, 29-35 (Syriac rubrics)

- **n413d** = John 1:51-2:3; 2:9-11
- **n150** = John 3:18-21, 26-27
- **n151 & n409** = Matthew 5:30-33, 38-41 (Syriac rubrics on n151)
- **n152** = Luke 13:3-4; Matthew 20:17-19
- **n153** = Luke 16:2-15; John 9:39 (Syriac rubrics)
- **n154** = Matthew 24:24-26, 32-33
- **n156** = Luke 24:19-32
- **n157** = Luke 24.32-5; John 15.18-21
- **n158** = Matthew 10:14-15, 16-33; John 20:19-25 (Syriac rubrics)
- **n413a1** = Matthew 10:19-20, 27 (joins with n158)
- **n413a2** = John 20:19, 25 (Syriac rubrics, joins with n158)
- **n413b** = John 14:11-12; 16:19
- **n159b** = small fragment from now lost folio containing John 17:24-6; Luke 24:36-47
- **n162** = Luke 10:34-42; 6:12-17 (Syriac rubrics)
- **n160** = John 9:9-23
- **n161** = John 9:23-38
- **n163** = Matthew 13:17-19, 24-25 (Syriac rubrics)
- **n164** = Matthew 25:45-46; 16:24-17:6 (Syriac rubrics)
- **n165 & n413c** = Luke 12:35-39, 42-44; John 5:19 (Syriac rubrics)

E6 = Syriac-Sogdian Pauline epistle lectionary[105]

- **n201** = Galatians 3:25-4:6
- **n200** = Titus 3:2-7; Romans 11:13-15
- **n202** = Romans 11:18-20, 22-23
- ***T II B [Y] & n203** = 1 Corinthians 5:7-8; 11:23-25
- **n204** = 1 Corinthians 1:24-25, 27-28
- **n398** = 1 Timothy 2:9-10, 14-15
- **n205, n206 & n411** = 1 Corinthians 12:13-21

· M I C H A E L   A Z A R ·

John Chrysostom and
the Johannine Jews

"For, it is the cause of all evils that many do not know how to use the testimonies of
Scripture rightly."

—Hom. Jo. 17

W ithin the plentitude of recent works on the Fourth Gospel
and anti-Judaism, John Chrysostom routinely serves as one,
if not the principal, example of the lamentable tale of Christian anti-Jewish polemics, to which the evangelist's words unwittingly
gave rise.[1] Few of these works, however, betray much familiarity with
either Chrysostom's *Homilies on John*[2] or his use of the gospel elsewhere. The purpose of this paper is to investigate specifically the function of the Johannine Jews in Chrysostom's Johannine homilies. As
such, what follows is not a comprehensive overview of the "Jews" in
Chrysostom's thought—that is for another time and another, still badly
needed, project.[3] Rather, the purpose here is exegetical: to explore
how Chrysostom, the great Antiochene preacher of the fourth century,
exegeted the Johannine Jews.

Understanding the function of mimesis and parenesis in Chrysostom's preaching provides the key to unraveling the role of the Jews—
or, indeed, any gospel character, including Jesus—in Chrysostom's
homilies. While many patristic writers harbored bitter feelings toward
their Jewish counterparts, as their Jewish counterparts did for them as
well, Chrysostom did not read John in the way so often assumed. Rather than read in order to shed light on the historical context of the
Fourth Gospel, Chrysostom—as nearly any other patristic writer
would—read in order to shed light on his own situation. In other
words, he read this text mimetically, with a parenetic outlook: he read
John as if John were written for him, referring directly to his own contemporary situation.

In the spiritual formation of his audience, Chrysostom presents his contemporary situation as a typological imitation of the pattern of events in John. In his exegesis, Christ's purposes are portrayed in such a way that they become identical to Chrysostom's own, and the shortcomings of the recipients of Christ's teaching, the Jews, become the apparent shortcomings of Chrysostom's contemporary ecclesial audience. Through such exegesis, through this mimetic correspondence—in which the fourth century appears to imitate the first century—Chrysostom continues the pedagogy of Jesus.[4] His parenetic concerns and mimetic approach remain, ultimately, why Chrysostom does not in fact read the Fourth Gospel against contemporary Jews.

Chrysostom and Christ as Teachers

Chrysostom's self-description of his primary role as a teacher—and how this role imitates the purpose and characteristics of the Christ whom he exegetes—comprises the first step to recognizing the mimetic features of Chrysostom's preaching. As he describes, he is a caring and persistent, even stubborn, teacher, and his audience his pupils, the fruit of his labor.[5] He struggles time and again because his pupils are frequently obstinate and easily offended at his tiresome and sharp words, but he persists, despite their open complaining.[6] In sum, his self-description presents a good, but tough teacher. Such is precisely his portrayal of Christ, the caring but tough teacher in the Fourth Gospel,[7] and thus we find revealed, though the twofold act of Chrysostom's exegesis and preaching, a mimetic correspondence between Christ and Chrysostom.

John's Jews and Chrysostom's Christians

Accordingly, Chrysostom's exegesis also reveals a mimetic correspondence between the teachers' pupils: Christ's pupils, the Jews of the gospel, and Chrysostom's pupils, his ecclesial community. In this way, the fourth and the first centuries "inter-illuminate" one another.[8] The deficiencies that Chrysostom perceives in his listeners and the parenetic demands that he places upon them mimetically parallel the same demands that Chrysostom understands Christ to be placing upon his Jewish listeners. Those demands correspond to three particular, inter-related vices with which Chrysostom indicts both the Johannine Jews and his contemporary community: 1) vainglory; 2) anger or envy, and 3) worldliness or materialism.

Vainglory/Conceit (κενοδοξία)

Chrysostom frequently accuses his listeners of vainglory and warns them of its dangers. He claims that it was "ambition to hold first place" (προεδίας ἐρᾶν) that had spawned heresies, and after describing the dangers of vainglory, he enjoins his listeners, "….let us flee this disease with all zeal and earnestness. Even if we have innumerable virtues, the plague of vainglory is capable of destroying them all."[9] Weeding his community of vainglory is one of his chief pastoral concerns in these homilies, and to lend to that end, he uncovers that the Jews in John imitate the vices present within his own community.

John the Evangelist does not specifically fault the Jews for their vainglory in many instances—the one certain example is in John 12, where the author observes, "Nevertheless, even many of the authorities believed in him, but because of the Pharisees they did not confess, in order that they might not be put out of the synagogue; for they loved the glory of people more than the glory of God" (Jn 12:42-43).[10] To be sure, Chrysostom seizes upon this opportunity to preach against vainglory, but besides this passage in John 12, there is little else in the gospel that lends to Chrysostom's unwavering claim that vainglory was the cause of the Jewish leaders' rejection. It is, rather, his *pastoral concern* for vainglory that leads Chrysostom to find this fault among the Jews of the gospel. And so, Chrysostom claims that the Jewish leaders, unlike the Apostles, fell because they were vain,[11] and the Jews in the gospel rejected Christ not because they were ignorant, but on account of their vainglory.[12]

Anger (ὀργή) and Envy (φθόνος)

In close proximity to vainglory, lies, for Chrysostom, two inseparable and equally troublesome vices: anger and envy. Both vices comprise the charge Chrysostom most frequently levies against the Johannine Jews, and, as such, Chrysostom causes the Johannine Jews to serve as negative paradigms of how his hearers ought not act.[13] In nearly every homily, he warns his hearers of the dangers of both envy and anger: Envy "is a venomous beast, an unclean beast, a defect of purpose, having no pardon, a vice deprived of a defense, the cause and mother of all evils."[14] Envy and anger, he says with regards to the Samaritan Woman, caused the Jews to drive Christ away while the Gentiles received him.[15] And, most disconcertingly, he claims, in Homily 48, that envy caused the Jews to become "Christ-killers" (χριστοκτόνοι).[16]

This last point is indeed troubling and conducive, perhaps, to the typical image of Chrysostom to which scholars frequently allude but rarely investigate, but Chrysostom's words elsewhere in these homilies with regards to the Jews and the effects of envy make it clear that this accusation speaks more to Chrysostom's understanding of envy than his understanding of anything unique to Jews as a whole.[17] For him, anger and envy are closely aligned, for the latter frequently leads to the former. Most readings of the Fourth Gospel may reveal a different reason that the Jews ultimately call for Jesus' crucifixion (such as his apparent blasphemy and disregard of the Torah), but for Chrysostom, it was their envy.[18]

Perhaps surprisingly, this accusation of "Christ-killer" is not without its mimetic correspondence within Chrysostom's own community. The conclusion of the immediately preceding homily (Homily 47) provides the only other instance where this appellation occurs. Even before Chrysostom wields this accusation against the Johannine Jews, he establishes who within his community are lost in the same way: He asks,

> Do you not betray Christ? When you neglect a poor man wasted with hunger, or perishing with cold, you are liable to the same sentence [as Judas]. And when we partake of the mysteries unworthily, we are lost in the same way as the Christ-killers. When we rob, when we strangle those who are weaker, we invite upon ourselves the greatest vengeance, and rightly so.[19]

Even in Homily 48, where Chrysostom asserts that envy led the Jews in John to become Christ-killers, it is evident that Chrysostom's exegesis is a product of his parenesis, and not vice versa. This homily concludes with a moral exhortation for his people to abandon the envy that leads to anger, which, he notes, is the same as madness (μανίας) and worse than demonic possession.[20] Chrysostom portrays the Jews as envious and angry not to vilify or defame the Jews *per se* (as he might in *Adversus Judaeos*), but to set up a paradigm with which to contend over envy and the anger that stems from it.

Worldliness/Materialism

Closely related to these vices of vainglory, envy, and anger, is that quibble for which Chrysostom is best known: his antipathy toward materialism and worldliness. As with vainglory, envy, and anger, Chrysostom's parenetic purposes with regards to materialism inform his exegetical endeavors. Whether it is prominence of family, lineage, or social status,[21] the possession of many things,[22] or worldly disposition,[23] Chrysostom discovers it present in the Jews of the Fourth Gospel. Such is the reason, according to Chrysostom, that on more than one occasion those who heard Jesus could not accept what he said: "....even if [Christ] had said nothing, they would have been scandalized and would not have ceased to be so, since their thoughts were always centered on bodily nourishment and attached to things of earth."[24]

Given that Chrysostom so frequently censures his hearers on account of their own materialistic desires and worldliness,[25] one need not go far to witness the mimetic correspondence: worldliness prevents the Jews in the gospel from fully grasping Christ's words as it does for Chrysostom's hearers as well. Still, Chrysostom recognizes this, and as Jesus chose his words carefully "because of the worldliness and weakness of the Jews" in order to make faith in him "easier to digest,"[26] so also Chrysostom explicitly feeds his hearers little by little to "make it easy" for them "to hold fast those things already given to [them]."[27]

Antiochene Exegesis and Mimetic Correspondence

To summarize: The twofold action of Chrysostom's exegesis and preaching set up a mimetic correspondence between his audience and the Johannine Jews that hinges upon Christ's and Chrysostom's roles as teachers and three particular shortcomings of their students: vainglory, envy or anger, and worldliness or materialism. Much like a modern critic, Chrysostom recognizes the importance of establishing the characteristics of the audience to whom Christ spoke if one is to understand the meaning of his words.[28] However, Chrysostom's Antiochene exegesis is far from being historical (at least in the modern, historical-critical sense).[29] He did not operate as if the text spoke of a time past, whose original meaning one must establish before one could apply it to the time now. Rather, Chrysostom's exegesis revolves around his parenetic intentions. The textual details he elucidates, and the manner in which he elucidates them, are shaped by the pastoral need that he perceives. The current situation and the spiritual formation that Chrysostom seeks in his hearers shape how he understands the messages of the text and, therefore, how he characterizes the Johannine Jews.[30]

This, ultimately, is what causes Chrysostom to make comparatively little of the fact that the people to whom Christ spoke in the gospel were primarily Jews.[31] That is not to say that his homilies do not contain any opposition toward Judaism: that is assuredly *not* the case, as he includes all of the basic patristic references regarding Jerusalem's destruction and Jewish unbelief, the Jews' failure to understand Christ on account of their overzealous concern for the Law, Jewish rejection and choosing of the Gentiles, and so forth. He faults Nicodemus for his "Jewish weakness";[32] he disparages the "Jewish insensitivity,"[33] and he notes the necessity of the disciples' own cleansing from their "Jewish error"[34]— all of which appear to mean that the Jews are too literalistic, failing to accept Christ's divinity and all that it entails. Nonetheless, the limitations that Chrysostom perceives in the Johannine Jews are most often generalized, beyond anything specific to Jews: His main issues are their misconceptions about the person of Christ, their ill dispositions and their vices. The problems he most often discovers in the text happen to be same problems he perceives within his own community.

Conclusion

Chrysostom's vehement opposition towards Jews and "Judaizers" is among the most famous in all of patristic literature. His *Adversus Judaeos* contains the most surprising and direct opposition to contemporary Jews, who themselves comprised a powerful, influential, and visible presence in Antioch. Although Chrysostom completed these homilies within a few years of his homilies on John, he does not typically use the material in the Fourth Gospel against contemporary Jewish opponents (nor does he make much use of this gospel in *Adversus Judaeos*). One would suspect that the material in John would provide ample fuel for the fire. In fact, though Chrysostom frequently and directly addresses his contemporaries in his homilies on John (usually the nefarious within his community but also heretics and pagans of various sorts[35]), he only directly addresses contemporary Jews once.[36]

Whatever Chrysostom's reasons, it is assuredly clear that he does not use the Fourth Gospel to vilify contemporary Jews, despite the usual scholarly assumption regarding the gospel's anti-Jewish reception history. Not even in his homilies on Christ's Passion does he attempt to defame Jews, because for him, the Passion does not serve to encourage opposition, violent or not, to contemporary Jews, as it would later in history, but as a call to endure suffering and opposition as did Christ.[37]

Nevertheless, Chrysostom indeed recognizes that the Fourth Gospel comprises a less than affable portrayal of the Jews. In commenting on the evangelist's final words regarding Jesus' many other deeds that could have been recorded, he paraphrases the evangelist's intentions:

> From this it is evident that [in writing] I was not currying favor. Though there were so many things that could have been written I did not even tell as many as the others. On the contrary, I omitted most of these and exposed, instead, the plotting of the Jews, the stoning, the hatred, the insults, the reviling, and revealed how they called Christ a demonic and seducer. It is very clear, therefore, that if I did all this, I was not trying to curry favor.[38]

Modern scholars, in a historically conscious mindset, frequently envision the Fourth Gospel's portrayal of the Jews as the Johannine community's addressing their Jewish contemporaries and expressing a deep sense of hostility caused by alienation.[39] However, Chrysostom, for whom parenesis shapes exegesis, understands John's portrayal of the Jews as indicative of the fact that John did not seek to curry favor.

The true opponents in Chrysostom's homilies, besides the various heretics and pagans, are the wealthy, the vainglorious, the angry, the miserly, the adulterous, the lazy, and such within his own community. In Chrysostom's estimation, the gospel was written to warn his audience, even directly, of such vices and to instruct them of the need for repentance and redemption through charity, the need not to be vengeful but to be willing to suffer much.[40] As he exhorts in the conclusion of Homily 49, "Let us think not that these words were spoken only to them then, but also to us, so that we may not corrupt justice in any matter but do everything in order to secure it."[41]

Theōria as a Hermeneutical Term in the Commentaries of Theodore of Mopsuestia and Theodoret of Cyrus

I n this chapter I attempt to define *theōria* (θεωρία)[1] and illustrate its use in two significant fourth and fifth century Antiochene church fathers. In particular this chapter provides such analysis of primary source material in the commentaries of Theodore of Mopsuestia and Theodoret of Cyrus.[2]

Significant research on Antiochene exegesis exists. But little of that research provides in depth study of *theōria* in the primary sources of Theodore and Theodoret. This chapter builds on the foundation of Bradley Nassif's dissertation, where he analyzes *theōria* mostly in the NT writings of John Chrysostom (along with secondary research from 1880 to 1990).[3] In this chapter I hope to help fill a lacunae on *theōria* in other Antiochene writings beyond John Chrysostom's.[4] Regarding such analysis the Catholic patristic scholar Bertrand de Margerie writes, "The complexity of the material available shows that we still undoubtedly await the definitive work that will give us an exact understanding of the meaning of Antiochian *theōria*, or, better still, of the different meanings of the term found in the authors of the School and even within the same author."[5]

It is important to understand the use of *theōria* in Antiochene exegesis because some treat it like nascent historical-critical (or historical-grammatical) interpretation (practically ignoring Antiochene *theōria*),[6] while others claim there is barely any distinction between Antiochene and Alexandrian exegesis.[7] In contrast, my research shows that *theōria* is a Spirit driven means whereby both Theodore and Theodoret locate links between the OT and the NT, as well as from the biblical text to the lives of their readers, while generally maintaining an integrated view of the textual and spiritual meaning.[8]

I attempt to show first that Theodore's exegesis has much in common with Chrysostom and Theodoret. Those distinctions are influenced by the continual interplay between theology and exegesis at the level of the discourse, and by a conviction that perception of the text's meaning is by means of study and the Spirit, among other factors. One key factor is the distinction between Antiochene *theōria* and Alexandrian *allēgoria* (ἀλληγορία). Interaction with the primary sources of Theodore and Theodoret seems to affirm that distinctions remain.[9] Of course the best way to prove such assertions for consensus between Antiochene exegetes is to show it in their extant writings.

Backgrounds of the Antiochenes
Theodore of Mopsuestia and Theodore of Cyrus

Prior to analysis of the commentaries of Theodore and Theodoret for their uses of *theōria* as a hermeneutical term, I provide a brief background study, first for Theodore, and then Theodoret, emphasizing their writings. A case has been made elsewhere that Theodore (350–428) and Theodoret (393–458) share a common training and social network that informs their theology and exegesis.[10] They both support Nicene orthodoxy and Theodoret spans the bridge of theological development to Chalcedon.[11]

Theodore's Background

The Antiochene patristic scholar Robert Hill says that Theodore pays Diodore his teacher "the sincerest form of flattery in more closely adhering to his exegetical principles."[12] Hill notes that one of those principles survives in a fragment of Diodore's *Quaestiones on the Octateuch*: "We (in Antioch) far prefer τὸ ἱστορικόν to τὸ ἀλληγορικόν (as practiced in Alexandria)." Hill then comments about this important Antiochene exegetical principle, that it "presumably suffuses his missing work on the difference between Antioch's favored hermeneutical approach of θεωρία and that of ἀλληγορία.[13]

Theodore faithfully serves the churches in his region, writings commentaries on most of the Bible as well as numerous *Catechetical Homilies* and a work on exegesis *On Allegory and History* (found during World War I but disappointingly lost soon after).[14] Theodore's extant biblical commentaries include those on Psalms 1–81 (in Greek and Latin),[15] on the Twelve (Minor) Prophets (in Greek),[16] on John (a fragmented Syriac translation and in the original Greek),[17] on some of the synoptic gospels and the Pauline Epistles (a fifth century Latin translation with some Greek fragments) as well as fragments of commentaries of Genesis and a little of Exodus.[18] Perhaps the most complete source of Theodore's extant Greek writings is found in the Thesaurus Linguae Graecae digital database (TLG). It includes material from his commentaries on Genesis, Psalms, the Twelve Prophets, Matthew, John, Acts (dubious?), Romans, 1 and 2 Corinthians, Hebrews, along with several other writings.[19]

Theodoret's Background

Theodoret (also Theodoretus) of Cyrus (also Cyr, Cyros, or Cyrrhus) serves as a Syrian Antiochene church leader a generation after Theodore. Theodoret has broad interests as an apologist, philanthropist, spiritual biographer, historian, monk, bishop, exegete and theologian. This background study focuses on his writings.

Theodoret is "educated in local monasteries and probably was not a pupil of Theodore. Nevertheless, he was deeply committed to the theology of the Antiochene school."[20] He claims Theodore and Diodore as his teachers through books.[21] Theodoret lives and ministers near Apamea for seven years before the appointment to his bishopric.[22] In 423 Theodoret is appointed bishop of the city of Cyrus—of the district of Cyrrhestica (Κυρρηστική)—about 75 miles east of Syrian Antioch.[23] There he serves 800 parishes, caring for the flocks and protecting them from such heresies as Marcionism, Arianism, and Eunomianism (ultra-Arians).[24] Theodoret suffers exile from his see in 449 not at the hands of the Alexandrians, but instead the Eutychians (monophysites or more accurately miaphysites).[25] He participates in the Council at Chalcedon, but only after affirming the anathemas on Nestorius and all who do not claim Mary as Θεοτόκος (*Theotokos*).[26]

Unlike Theodore (who, with all his writings, is condemned posthumously), the Second Council at Constantinople (553) only condemns a couple of Theodoret's writings including *Refutation of Cyril's Twelve Anathemas*.[27] Therefore, Theodoret's extant writings are extensive.[28] Since the focus of this chapter is on his exegetical methods, only his biblical commentaries are listed here. TLG lists ten Greek sources for Theodoret ("Theodoretus") which provide commentaries on forty-four books of the Bible.[29]

In the preface to his *Commentary on the Psalms*[30] Theodoret notes that he had already written his *Commentary on the Song of Songs*.[31] He also writes commentaries on Daniel,[32] Ezekiel,[33] Jeremiah,[34] *Commentary on the Twelve Prophets* (PG, 81.1545–58) prior to his *Commentary on the Psalms*,[35] and *The Questions on the Octateuch*[36] as well as a work on the biblical books of Samuel, Kings and Chronicles.

In the following section I use the TLG database to locate relevant texts from Theodore's and Theodoret's commentaries to analyze their uses of *theōria* and *theōreo* in the original contexts and in order to determine a range of meanings for the terms.

Analysis of Theodore's Commentaries

Searching the TLG digital database[37] under all available sources for "Theodorus Mopsuestenus" reveals fifteen instances of the term *theōria* in its various cases and numbers. The search also reveals thirty-six instances of the verb *theōreo*. The following analysis includes only discussion of these terms in Theodore's writings which underscore hermeneutical significance.[38] The following analysis focuses especially on Theodore's commentaries on Psalms, the Twelve Prophets and the Gospel of John.

Commentary on Psalms

Despite Diodore's use of the term *theōria* many times in the preface to his *Commentary on Psalms*, Theodore does not mimic his mentor.[39] For Theodore never uses the term in his *Com. on Psalms 1–81*.[40] Scholars note that Theodore only acknowledges Christological interpretation in Psalm 2, 8, 44 (LXX; 45 in the MT and English) and 110.[41] For example in his *Com. on Psalms* for Psalm 69:10 he gives not a hint of Christological interpretation. Nevertheless, in his *Com. on Joel* Theodore's interpretation is freer. There he continues to acknowledge a near referent, but now adds another "more real" (far) referent found in Psalm 69:10.

> Blessed David likewise says about the people, "Its soul was not abandoned to Hades, nor did its flesh see corruption," which cannot be understood at

the level of fact [πραγμάτων]; rather, by the use of hyperbole [ὑπερβολικῶς] or metaphor [μεταφορικῶς] he says it was rescued from danger or corruption. The factual reality of the text [ἡ δὲ τοῦ πράγματος ἀλήθεια τῶν εἰρημένων], on the other hand, is demonstrated by Christ the Lord, when it happened that neither was his soul abandoned to Hades, being restored to the body in the resurrection, nor did his body suffer any corruption, so that not only did it remain with its own appearance in which is actually died but it was also transformed into an immortal and incorruptible nature.[42]

Theodore says that the near (that is Jewish) referent for Psalm 69:10 cannot be understood factually, but hyperbolically (ὑπερβολικῶς) or metaphorically (μεταφορικῶς).[43] In other words, the passage is not fully actualized in the near Jewish referent. But the realization of hyperbole in the text leads the interpreter to find "the factual reality of the text" (i.e., the true or ultimate referent) in Christ Jesus.[44]

Similarly Theodore acknowledges in his *Com. on Micah* 5:2 that Psalm 89:30–33 clearly relates hyperbolically to the descendants of David, but in full reality to Jesus Christ. For Theodore the passage cannot speak literally of David's descendants for that would overstate historical realities. But it can be taken literally for Christ Jesus.

You could grasp this more clearly from the eighty-eighth Psalm [LXX], where it indicates that the promises of kingship apply to . . . the future descendants of David. . . . He [the psalmist] proceeds, however, to foretell Christ the Lord according to the flesh, in whose case God demonstrated the true fulfillment of his promise: "I shall establish his offspring forever and ever, and his throne as long as the heavens last." . . . Thus you would see the present testimony applying in one case in the true and indisputable proof from experience in the case of Christ the Lord, in keeping with the statement in the Gospels, kings of Israel from David being cited on account of the divine promise.[45]

Therefore, while Theodore appears to interpret rather literally and within a narrow OT time-frame that disallows many messianic or typological readings in his *Com. on Psalms*, when he comments on the Psalms elsewhere he is more likely to acknowledge those messianic or typological connections. Scholars should therefore acknowledge at least *six* Psalms for which Theodore acknowledges a messianic referent (2, 8, 45, 69, 89, 110).

Commentary on the Twelve Prophets

Theodore affirms Peter's use of Joel 2:28–32, "since the Law contained a shadow of the things to come. . . . What happened in their time was all insignificant and like shadow so that the account was given with use of hyperbole rather than containing facts, whereas the reality of the account was found to be realized in the time of Christ the Lord."[46] Theodore is clearly not arguing against the historical reality of OT events, nor denying the truthfulness of the OT narrative. Instead, he emphasizes that when hyperbole is used by an OT author, the OT events are like shadows and insignificant *relative* to their fulfillment in Christ Jesus. Theodore sees such interpretation as requiring *theōria*. His discussion on Nahum 1:1 bears this out.[47]

Theodore's comments on Nahum 1:1 contains his densest use of *theōria*, where he uses the term eight times.[48] For example, he notes that the prophets by receiving such visions were "enabled to be attentive completely to the contemplation [*theōria*] of the revelations."[49] For Theodore, *theōria* is a significant aspect of a prophet's musing over a revelation or a vision.[50] He explains by example:

> After all, it is not possible for us to gain precise learning from our mentors unless we distance ourselves from everything and with great assiduity give heed to what is said, how would it have been possible for them [OT prophets] to be the beneficiaries of such awesome and ineffable contemplation [*theōria*; PG 66.401.51] without first being removed in their thinking from reality [*theōria*; PG 66.401.53] on that occasion?[51]

To effectively contemplate the vision, the prophet could not at the same time contemplate earthly realities occurring around him. Thus, the Greek has *theōria* (in the plural) twice, and Hill translates it as "contemplation" only the first time, but with the more mundane "thinking from reality" the second.[52] Next Theodore illustrates *theōria* in the NT.

> This is the way Scripture says blessed Peter was in an ecstatic state and saw the cloth let down from heaven: since the grace of the Spirit first distanced his mind of reality, then it caused him to be devoted to the contemplation [*theōria*; PG 66.404.1] of the revelations and so, just as we are beyond our normal condition as though asleep when we receive contemplation [*theōria*; PG 66.404.4] of what is revealed, so in some fashion they were affected by a transformation of mind from the Holy Spirit and became beneficiaries of the contemplation [*theōria*; PG 66.404.6] of the revelations.[53]

Theodore has already used *theōria* for OT prophets (PG 66.401.47, 51, 53; 404.6). Here he applies it first to Peter (and by extension all NT authors; 404.1, 6, citing Acts 10:11–12), and to his contemporaries ("we"; 404.4). That is, Theodore uses *theōria* to describe not only the OT prophets and NT apostles contemplating a vision received, *but also for post-New Testament believers contemplating the received revelation of Scripture* ("just as we are beyond our normal condition as though asleep when we receive contemplation [PG 66.404.4] of what is revealed").[54] "As though asleep" may seem to imply that Theodore promotes ecstatic trances to gain insight to Scripture. But from what is known of his strong rational emphasis, it seems more appropriate to understand this phrase as an illustration of the recipient/exegete completely devoted to the contemplation of the revelation.[55] This rational emphasis does not, however, deny for Theodore a role for the Holy Spirit in contemplation (as he already stated above). Namely, the Spirit first distances the mind of physical realities, and then the Spirit causes the recipient/exegete to be devoted to or focused on the contemplation.

The Spirit's role in contemplation is seen, for example, as Theodore concludes his comments on Nahum 1:1 with two uses of the term *theōria* applied specifically to Nahum.

> The prophet's mind was suddenly seized by the grace of the Spirit and transformed so as to contemplate [*theōria*; PG 66.404.47] those things through which he learnt of the fate of Nineveh and that he provided to his listeners as instruction in what was shown to him. Hence the mention of *oracle* and *vision*, in order to indicate by the former the manner of the activity of the Holy Spirit, and by *vision*, the contemplation [*theōria*; PG 66.404.52] of what was shown to him.[56]

Without the Holy Spirit Theodore does not see other effective means for scriptural contemplation. While emphasizing the role of the Spirit in *theōria*, effective contemplation "by the grace of the Spirit" is also for Theodore more available to "those thought worthy of such things."[57] Yet who is worthy of such grace?

Commentary on John's Gospel

In John's Gospel Theodore considers the greatness of God's grace in sending His unique Son. He comments on Jesus' words in John 12:44–45, "whoever sees me, sees him who sent me": "For the one who through this one [Christ Jesus] perceives [*theōreo*] that person

[God the Father], through the likeness [Christ Jesus] by *theōria* is introduced [προσάγω]."[58] Phillip wants to meet this Father about whom Jesus speaks. But Jesus tells him (and the others) that without discerning (*theōreo*) the likeness of God (Jesus Christ) one cannot be introduced to the Father. How such discernment is possible, Theodore explains in his *Com. on Zechariah* (1:8–11).

> Elsewhere the Lord says more clearly to them, "I have told you this in parables, but I will openly report to you on the Father," bringing out that they had heard word of the Father obscurely . . . but they would truly know the Son when they know him to be God in his being, coming from him, and one in being with him. . . . Hence also the Lord says to them, "I have many things yet to say, but you cannot bear them now; when that Spirit of truth comes, however, he will guide you in all truth."[59]

So for Theodore the disciples cannot know the Father without truly knowing the Son of God. And they know "the Son when they know him to be God in his being, coming from him, and one in being with him." Such perception for Theodore is only possible when the Spirit of truth comes (John 16:12). Thus again Theodore shows that such discernment or ability to perceive (*theōria*) requires Holy Spirit enablement.[60]

But Theodore's brief comments on John 14:17 are perhaps still more significant. The text is worth quoting in full.

> You are destined to partake of the Spirit; and so great is the giving of the Spirit that, if it [the Holy Spirit] does not wish it, the whole *world cannot seize* it to itself. He did not say "receive" but "seize", as if to get a hold of it. "You see", He says, "if someone can neither see [θεωρῆσαί] it nor know it, how could it be seized by them? Accordingly, you will come to know the Spirit, and also have it in you, through me." However, He did not also say, "You will see [ὄψεσθε]" for this is impossible.[61]

Theodore understands that the Holy Spirit is incorporeal and therefore invisible. Thus to physically see (ὁράω) the Holy Spirit is impossible. But for Theodore, neither can one perceive (θεωρέω) the Holy Spirit, unless one is—like those chosen apostles—"destined to partake of the Spirit." [62] This is by the grace of God.

In summary, Theodore understands *theōria* as insight by vision, as contemplation of a vision, revelation, or text of revelation, and as a perceiving of spiritual truths enabled by the Holy Spirit. This concludes the use of *theōria* and *theōreo* by Theodore. The discussion now turns to Theodoret's use of these terms and then a brief comparison of the two Antiochenes' uses of these terms.

Analysis of Theodorete's Commentaries

Because many more of Theodoret's exegetical writings remain, it is not surprising that a search of the biblical commentaries of Theodoret ("Theodoretus") in the TLG reveals 79 instances of *theōria* in its various cases and numbers—considerably more than for Theodore. The TLG also reveals 121 instances of verbal variants of *theōreo* from these same ten sources.[63] Fewer of these, however, offer important insight into Antiochene *theōria* as an exegetical method. Nevertheless, Theodoret does significantly use the terms, though not always following the same theoretic process of his Antiochene mentors Theodore and Diodore.

For Theodoret, physical eyes are insufficient to perceive spiritual truth—though they can provide a stepping stone to the latter. So physical eyes (and discerning minds) may provide insight, for example, from the resulting calamities for people who do not live holy lives.[64] And a holy life grants greater perception into God and His Word.[65] Theodoret's use of *theōria* and *theōreo* are organized by commentary as follows.

Commentary on The Psalms

Theodoret uses the term *theōria* seven times in his *Com. on Psalms*. From Psalm 19:1 he compares the sight (*theōria*) of a painting with the sight of creation. As the former brings to mind the painter, so the latter brings to mind the creator.[66] This may seem like a distinct use from his *Com. on Ezekiel* where he emphasizes repeatedly that a spiritual vision (not to mention God the Father or Spirit) cannot be seen by natural eyes. But for Theodoret, though natural eyes cannot see the invisible (namely, God), they do provide the ability to see the visible, which *images* or points to the invisible.

Theodoret uses the term *theōria* in his comments on Psalm 81:11–12 (LXX 80:12–13), writing, "The truth of the inspired composition is available for the discernment [*theōria*] of those ready for it." So grasping the thrust of the passage only comes for those prepared.[67] Robert Hill understands such use of *theōria* as that which "enables the reader of the psalm to find a fuller sense in reference to the Jews of [Theodoret's] day."[68] He apparently draws this conclusion from Theodore's introduction to "this Psalm [which] prophesies the recall of the Jews." But Theodoret also sees this Psalm prophesying of Jewish "estrangement [from God] occurring after that" as well as "the calling of the nations."[69] Thus, Hill's notion of a "fuller sense" for *theōria* seems foreign to Theodoret's use of the term here. Instead, he appears to see these all as multiple referents of the one meaning of the passage.[70]

Regardless of the fuller sense versus multiple references debate, Theodoret clearly sees *theōria* as integral to interpretation of the passage. And this use of *theōria* and especially the verb *theōreo* appears a few other times in his *Com. on the Psalms*. For example, after his comments on Psalm 68:28–29, Theodoret concludes, "Eyes that perceive [*theōreo*] the realization of the prophecy are witnesses to this."[71] Thus, for Theodoret Psalm 68:29 prophesies of the incarnate Christ—for those with "eyes that perceive" Christ there. But Theodoret implies that all do not perceive this,[72] and those that do require assistance by the Holy Spirit.

Theodoret, commenting on "In your light we shall see light" in Psalm 36:9, writes, "illumined by the all-Holy Spirit we shall perceive [*theōreo*] the rays of your Only-begotten: Scripture says, "No one can say Jesus is Lord except by the Holy Spirit." We have consequently come to a precise knowledge of the three persons in the one divinity through the inspired words."[73] Thus Theodoret affirms the need for illumination by the Holy Spirit in order to perceive Jesus as Lord and the Trinity "through the inspired words." Theodoret's understanding of *theōria* as interpretive perception seems connected to a canonical reading of the text. So for example, commenting on Psalm 102:27, "You, on the contrary, are the same, and your years will not fail," Theodoret writes:

> so you remodel creation as you wish, O Lord; you have an immutable nature, proof against change. The divine Apostle, of course, attributes these verses to the particular characteristic of the Son in the Epistle to the Hebrews; yet likewise we discern [*theōreo*] the Father in the Son: for whatever he does the Son likewise does, and sameness of nature is recognized in each, for the operation of the Trinity is one, as we know.[74]

Theodoret refers here not only to Hebrews 1:10–12, but also to Jesus' words that if you have seen me you have seen the Father (John 14:9).

But Hill's comment—that Theodoret looks for a "fuller sense" by way of the process of *theōria*—rings true in the latter's comments on Psalm 46:8–9.

> The verse, *bringing wars to an end as far as the ends of the earth. He will break the bow, smash weapons, and burn shields in fire*, was thus fulfilled in a historical [κατὰ τὴν ἱστορίαν] sense; but if you wanted to understand it in a more figurative way [τροπικώτερον], you would have regard for the cessation of hostilities against the Church and the peace provided them from God, and you would perceive [θεωρήσει; *theōreo*] the realizations [ἀλήθειαν] of the prophecy.[75]

Theodoret, as Theodore before him, views all of the Psalms as prophetic.[76] But Theodoret freely suggests to his readers prophetic referents not only in the post-exilic period, but also post-apostolic.[77] *Theōreo* is necessary to achieve Theodoret's "more figurative" (τροπικώτερον) prophetic referent.[78]

Commentary on Songs

Theodoret in this, his first, exegetical work understandably displays more dependence on the works of others. Yet he often eschews the Antiochene approach of his schooling.[79] He provides several pages explaining why in his preface. He gives "thanks to the Spirit" for "entrance in spirit" to an interpretation of the Song which allows one to "behold the glory of the Lord with face unveiled" rather than by "a corporeal interpretation . . . [being] drawn into . . . awful blasphemy."[80] Theodoret also points to the figurative nature of the OT requiring figurative interpretation, in keeping with his rhetorical training.[81] Perhaps the echoes of anathemas from the Council of Ephesus (431) along with his ascetic sensibilities have also overcome his Antiochene historicism—leading to his most allegorical biblical exegesis.[82] Such motivation results in considerable divergence from Theodore in Theodoret's use of the terms *theōria* and *theōreo* in his *Com. on Song*.

Theodoret's preface starts with a description of prerequisites to the exegetical task not so foreign to Antiochene norms. "The explanation of the divine sayings requires, on the one hand, a purified soul that is also rid of every uncleanness; on the other hand, it requires as well a mind that has wings, capable of discerning [*theōria*] divine things and prepared to enter the precincts of the Spirit."[83] Thus, a pure heart and Antiochene *theōria*—described as a virtuous mental and Spirit-driven endeavor—are necessary prerequisites to interpretation. Theodoret readily admits his reliance on God for the work, and in particular for the illumination of the Holy Spirit, citing David's Psalm 119:18: "Take the veil from my eyes and I shall understand the wonders of your Law."[84]

With Antiochene precision (ἀκρίβεια) Theodoret explains the title "The Song of Songs" rather than a Song, because nothing in God's Holy Word is superfluous.[85] Yet Theodoret's remarks in the body of his commentary reveal an atypical Antiochene approach. While Theodoret makes links to antecedent OT theology (for example, promises made to Abraham and Moses' prophecies concerning the Bridegroom), never does he intimate that the bridegroom is other than the Lord, the Father's "Only-begotten Son."[86] Theodoret also makes use of later prophets like Hosea to support his immediate referencing of the bridegroom to the Son of God.[87] And this is typical throughout his commentary. He is just as comfortable making direct links to the NT. For example, Theodoret hesitates only briefly, interpreting "your name" in Song 1:3 to "Christ, as it were" and "your anointing oils" immediately refer to the Lord anointed with the Spirit.[88]

He finds in Song 1:6 not a woman left in the vineyards too long—thus darkened from the sun who fears rejection from her lover—but a reference to "an alien" who "because of her former superstition . . . had contracted a black colour." And thus "those who gloried in the Law and exalted themselves under the Old Covenant" despised her. Theodoret finds a comparison in Moses' marriage to a Cushite woman in Numbers 12:1–2.[89]

Often Theodoret's comments are unsupported by any biblical passages. For example, rather than the beloved bride in Song 1:8 receiving invitation to pasture her young goats at the tents of her bridegroom, Theodoret has the bride (who seeks her desire in the Lord) "examin[ing] the lives of the saints. . .in the tents of those shepherds, that is, in the Apostolic churches, [where she is encouraged to] feed thy kids." Apparently this is a reference to a new believer's children.[90]

Theodoret admits more hesitancy in his comments at times. For example he prefaces his comments on Song 1:11 with "they seem to signify" and he explains "our bed" in Song 1:16 with "He appears to intend Holy Scripture, in which the Bridegroom and Bride reposing have spiritual intercommunion."[91] Elsewhere he offers two interpretations, apparently unsure which is correct.[92] All in all, allegorization fills the commentary where in 3:4 the "city" is the "Church," "streets and ways" are the Holy Scriptures, "keepers of the city" refer to the "Holy Prophets and Apostles," and "mother's house and chamber" is heavenly Jerusalem.[93]

In his comments on Song 4:9—"You have captivated my heart, my sister, my bride; you have captivated my heart with one glance of your eyes"—Theodoret refers to *theōria*. He comments: "Both thine *eyes* are indeed admirable and spiritual, and to be called like dove's, but that one amazes me which contemplates [*theōria*] Divine things, which is skilled in researches of God, and sees the hidden mysteries."[94] Here Theodoret finds the Bridegroom favoring the bride's eye "which contemplates divine things." But his use of *theōria* becomes still more questionable. For example, in his commentary on Song 4:14 for the phrase "orchard of pomegranates" he ventures the explanation, "in my view pomegranate is to be taken figuratively [τροπικῶς] as love, since countless seeds are contained together within the one skin, pressed together without squeezing or ruining one another, remaining fresh unless one of the seeds in the middle goes bad." Then to his figurative (allegorical) interpretation, Theodoret now recommends "insight" (*theōria*) by interpreting each seed in the pomegranate as a class of people in the church.[95]

Theodoret does seek to gain some discernment (*theōria*) "not only from the translation of the word, but also from the word itself" and so recommends for Song 7:2 inquiry "into the identity of Nadab."[96] This use of *theōria* seems more in keeping with typical Antiochene emphases on ἱστορία and precision (ἀκρίβεια).

Commentary on Isaiah

Theodoret uses the term *theōria* three times in his *Com. on Isaiah*. The first two are located in his comments on Isaiah 12:5–6. There he references Moses' raising of the bronze serpent for the healing of the sinful Israelites in Numbers 21:5 as well as Jesus' discussion of it in John 8:28 "When you have lifted up the Son of Man, then you will know that I am he." And again, "just as Moses lifted up the serpent in the desert, so must the Son of man be lifted up" (John 3:14). To these verses he adds the comment "And we who have believed in him look up in order that just as the Jews with the sight [theōria] of the bronze serpent dulled the work of poisonous snakes, so we with a vision [theōria] to him may be healed."[97] Here Theodoret uses theōria in both its more mundane (physical or literal) sense and more significant (spiritual) sense, drawing the connection from the type to its antitype in the crucifixion and glorification of the Lord Jesus Christ.

Commentary on Ezekial

Theodoret untiringly explains the nature of Ezekiel's visions as spiritual and not perceptible with the human eye. For example, in Ezekiel 1:2 he comments, "Now, he said 'the heavens opened,' not in actual fact but in a spiritual insight [theōria]." This relates to Theodoret's high view of the transcendence of God's essence. Unlike Theodore, Theodoret displays a much looser interpretation, linking Ezekiel's receiving a vision by the river Chebar (Ezekiel 1:3) with NT regeneration of all peoples.[98] But Theodoret's use of theōria in his comments on Ezekiel 3:22 is especially reminiscent of Theodore's comments on Nahum 1:1. Theodoret writes, "Isolation is suited to the vision [theōria] of divine things: the mind is rid of external distractions and no longer caught up in this direction and that, concentrating on itself and capable of closer appreciation of divine things." It seems clear that Theodoret himself has experienced this way of studying the Scripture.[99]

Along with quiet contemplation (theōria), Theodoret appeals to his readers for purity of life in keeping with the subject of these contemplations. For he notes (in his comments on Ezekiel 11:24b) that though Ezekiel was seated with the elders, "only the prophet received the spiritual vision [theōria]." Then he exhorts his readers. "May we, too, be zealous to attain this purity and ask for it, so that freed from every stain we may in the present life . . . constantly carry . . . the memory of God, and . . . be found worthy . . . to see him with confidence."[100] Theodoret links theōria to his readers (as Theodore does when commenting in Nahum 1:1, applying theōria to OT prophets, Peter and Theodore's contemporaries).[101] For Theodoret, such elevated visions cannot be attained without purity of life, neither for an OT prophet nor for a modern reader.[102]

Theodoret uses *theōria* to find applications for his contemporaries from the text. But in so doing he does not always give up the literal reading of the text for the theoretical. So for example, commenting on Ezekiel 39:29, Theodoret questions the "Jewish" interpretation that "the incursion of Gog and Magog did not already happen." Such interpreters "ought realize, firstly, that this man's prophecy is associated with the recall from Babylon; then, that in it he said that the nations would come to know God's power." He continues, that from God's teaching "we discern [θεωροῦμεν] the three persons in the one nature."[103] Theodoret shows concern for both a historical and spiritual reading.

Commentary on Daniel

When Theodoret uses the term *theōria* in his *Commentary on Daniel*, he generally means vision.[104] But he uses *theōria* here as insight, which can also be understood as perception or "understanding . . . like the gods"—words Belshazzar's queen uses to describe Daniel in Daniel 5:11. Theodoret comments that this is akin to Daniel having "insight [*theōria*] into what escaped many."[105]

New Testament Epistles Commentaries

Theodoret's more helpful uses of the term *theōria* and *theōreo* are in his *Com. on Hebrews*. The text of Hebrews 8:5, "They serve as a shadow and copy of the heavenly things," raises a question in Theodoret's mind. "If the priesthood according to the Law . . . came to an end . . . and made further sacrifices unnecessary, why do the priests of the New Covenant perform the sacramental liturgy?" This is a weighty question not about OT types but NT antitypes. Theodoret answers that "It is clear to those versed in divine things . . . that it is not another sacrifice we offer; rather, we perform the commemoration [μνήμης] of the one, saving sacrifice." This is as the Lord requires "so that we should recall with insight [*theōria*] the type of the suffering undergone for us, kindle love for the benefactor [God] and look forward to the enjoyment of the good things to come [heaven]."[106] So for Theodoret the purpose of the Lord's Table is to commemorate Christ's work on the cross. But this requires insight (*theōria*).[107]

And this insight for Theodoret comes by faith. So, commenting on Hebrews 10:19–22, he says that approaching the "invisible . . .

innermost sanctuary of the tabernacle . . . [is properly] discerned [*theōreo*] only through the eyes of faith." And again on Hebrews 11:1: "through it [faith] we see what is unseen, and it acts as an eye for discernment [*theōria*] of what is hoped for."[108]

Is such discernment simply a Greek patristic way of speaking, which is foreign to Scripture? I think not. The uses of the terms (*theōria* and *theōreo*) are limited in the NT. But the author of Hebrews does use *theōreo* in Hebrews 7:4. "See how great this man was to whom Abraham the patriarch gave a tenth of the spoil!" The verb "see" ("notice" in Hill's translation) is an imperative of *theōreo*. And like the biblical author of Hebrews, Theodoret—commenting on Hebrew 13:11–12—commands his readers to "look at the type, compare it with the reality and perceive [*theōreo*] the similarity." He follows this with a description of the typological similarities.[109] Theodoret wants his readers to turn their attention to the type, with the result that they *perceive* the intended comparison between the type (in the OT) and antitype (Christ in the NT). With such a command in the Bible, it is not surprising that Antiochene *theōria* has been linked to typology.[110]

In summary, for Theodoret *theōria* and *theōreo* describe a physical sight; discernment of or insight into usually a typological link, or (other times) an application; and spiritual perceiving usually requiring faith, Holy Spirit enablement or both.

Comparing Theodore's and Theodorete's *Theōria* Usage

The amount of material available for all of Theodore's writings (mostly exegetical) is one third of the extant exegetical material for Theodoret.[111] Yet Theodoret uses the word *theōria* almost twice as much as Theodore, *relative* to the total word count for each.[112] Probably this occurs because Theodoret's commentaries on OT apocalyptic books like Daniel and Ezekiel remain, while those from Theodore do not. Their uses of the term *theōreo* are comparable with only a ten percent relative increase for Theodoret's use over Theodore's.[113]

Both Theodore and Theodoret use *theōria* to describe a spectacle, visual observation, mental discernment, contemplation and spiritual or prophetic perception (usually of a vision or some other revelation). Both acknowledge the role of the Holy Spirit, as well as the necessity of the perceiver's complete attention for effective contemplation. Theodoret more fully develops the importance of the perceiver's spiritual condition, apparently a result of the availability of three times more extant commentaries from which to hear his views on *theōria*. Nothing in Theodore's writings indicates that he would disagree with Theodoret here.

Both Antiochenes affirm *theōria* as a contemplative and interpretive process for OT prophets, NT apostles as well as for the Antiochenes' contemporaries. Similarly, both Theodore and Theodoret use *theōreo* as the act of discerning or contemplating truth in visions (for OT prophets especially), in biblical events, and in the biblical text itself.

Theodoret, however, uses the terms far more freely to promote figurative (τροπικῶς) and at times allegorical (ἀλληγορικόν) interpretation—seen most acutely in his *Com. on Song*. This is clearly the strongest difference between Theodore and Theodoret.[114] Theodore did not write a full length commentary on that biblical book. His comments are limited to a letter "which indicates that he regards the Canticle of Canticles as Solomon's reply to the opponents of his marriage with the Egyptian princess and refuses to grant it any allegorical significance."[115] Instead, Theodore describes allegorical interpretation as "overturning the meaning of the divine Scriptures" and "fabricat[ing] from themselves . . . foolish fictions and . . . folly." Theodore rejects allegorical interpretation by the authority of Paul's comments in Galatians 4:24–30, because allegorical interpretation "dismiss[es] the entire meaning of divine Scripture . . . [while] the apostle does not do away with the narrative [ἰστορία] nor does it do away with what happened long ago."[116]

Does Theodoret's *Com. on Song* betray a fundamental Antiochene hermeneutic? At times, yes it does. But as a mature bishop, writing his *Com. on the Letters of Saint Paul*,[117] Theodoret appears to return to his Antiochene roots. Commenting on Galatians 4:24a "This is meant allegorically," Theodoret writes, "The divine apostle said *meant allegorically* to suggest it is to be understood differently: without cancelling the historical sense, he brings out what is prefigured [προτυπωθέντα] in the historical sense."[118] Theodoret's understanding of Paul's "This is meant allegorically" might correspond best with what biblical scholars today call typology. In his comments on verses 24–30 Theodoret uses the term τύπος ("type") four times, describing

Paul's "allegory" and concludes, "He [Paul] quotes Sarah's words [in verse 30], Scripture's words to bring out Scripture's purpose, that this was written so that the type might be revealed even after the facts."[119] So for Theodoret, Paul is not allegorizing but typologizing.[120]

Typologizing does not deny the original events occurred. It does not demand that the type be (fully) realized initially in the Scripture, though it lay there latently as a "prefigure." The original text and discourse has its own σκοπός (objective) that a type should not disintegrate. But the type is revealed "after the facts" of OT Scripture. The types that were once only latent in the OT are now revealed by the Christ event, about which Paul the inspired author writes in Galatians 4. Now the OT passages are like foreshadows (σκιά) in comparison to the NT realities. And now the reader with discernment (theōria) can see the relationship between the Testaments.[121]

Theodore is uncomfortable with figurative interpretation (τροπικῶς), but Theodoret employs it regularly—with a goal of showing the connection between the Testaments (especially as related to Christ or the Trinity or sometimes the church). But simultaneously Theodoret endeavors to affirm the σκοπός and ἰστορία along with Theodore, especially in his later writings. Thus Peter Gorday calls Theodoret "the archrepresentative of Antiochene exegesis."[122] So Theodoret wanders furthest from a normally historical reading (i.e., Antiochene reading) in his *earliest* commentary, while Theodore expresses more freedom in seeing Christological referents in OT passages *later* in his writing ministry.

It is not surprising that this synchronic analysis of the use of the terms *theōria* and *theōreo* in the commentaries of Theodore and Theodoret has led to some divergent semantic ranges. Nassif suggests that such might be the case; otherwise the study could have ended with his one contribution from the writings of John Chrysostom.[123] Furthermore, Schor reminds us that "even when scholars have original Greek terms, they find plenty of variation in word choice. And [even] word consistency may mask shifts of meaning between people and over time."[124] Nevertheless, this study has led to a relatively consistent understanding of the term for Theodore and Theodoret.

They both understand *theōria* and *theōreo*, when used as hermeneutical terms, as the contemplative interpretive process enabled by the Holy Spirit and applicable for OT prophets, for NT apostles, as well as for post-canonical interpreters who have faith to see. Similarly for John Chrysostom, Nassif concludes that *theōria* is broadly defined as "the divine revelation or mystical illumination of spiritual realities which attends the process of inscripturation, interpretation, or homiletical discourse within the framework of Incarnation history." Focusing on to the interpretive aspect of Antiochene *theoria*, Nassif summarizes that "the Spirit's activity in *theōria* can be observed in . . . interpretation . . . [as] the hermeneutical activity of the Holy Spirit in illuminating the understanding of the OT, NT or post-apostolic exegete."[125]

• VAHAN S. HOVHANESSIAN •

The Commentary of St. Ephrem the Syrian on the Apocryphal Third Corinthians

T he impressive number of surviving manuscripts containing the Classical Armenian translation of the writings of the fourth-century prolific Syrian poet, theologian, hymn writer and musician, St. Ephrem (circa 306–373), is an indication of the popularity of this saint among the Armenians and of the influence of the Syrain Church on the theology and liturgy of the Armenian Church.[1] St. Ephrem's interpretation of verses and pericopes in the various books of the Bible are also found commonly fused into the anthologies of biblical scholia of the Armenian Church fathers.[2]

Of special interest to our study is the several folios preserved in a collection of commentaries on the letters of St Paul attributed to St. Ephrem which survive only in Armenian manuscripts. These folios contain a commentary (henceforth, *the commentary*) on an apocryphal correspondence between St Paul and the Corinthians, known as *Third Corinthians* (3 Cor).[3] In the following pages of this paper we will focus on these folios and the comments they contain. The importance of this commentary, which is attributed to St. Ephrem, is manifold. First, the commentary on 3 Cor, as in the commentaries attributed to St. Ephrem on the other letters of St Paul, preserve the theology of the Aramaic-speaking people prior to the influence of Byzantium and the Western philosophy and theology. Secondly, the commentary can be used to reestablish and analyze the text of the apocryphal 3 Cor, because it represents the version of 3 Cor that was used by the author of the commentary. Finally the commentary survives only in the Armenian translation, and because of this most of its contents has been unknown to the majority of the scholars in the West.

The commentary has been traditionally attributed to St. Ephrem the Syrian. This is what almost all the Armenian manuscripts state. During the past century the authenticity of the authorship has been questioned by some scholars proposing that it may be a pseudepigraphic writing attributed intentionally to the fourth century prolific Syrian theologian. The examination of the identity of the author of the commentary is beyond the scope of our study. Because of this, we will use the phrase "the author" interchangeably with "Ephrem" in this article referring to the author of the commentary.

Very little attention has been given in the West to the Armenian translations of the commentaries attributed to St. Ephrem on the letters of the Apostle Paul. During the past century or so, the paucity of the scholarly work on these commentaries in Armenian is indeed startling. During the first half of the twentieth century two articles explored these commentaries. Joseph Schäfers investigated the Gospel citations in the Armenian translation of Ephrem's commentary on Paul's letters in his article published in 1917.[4] He concluded that the biblical quotations in the Armenian translation were based on a Syriac original. In 1937, Joseph Molitor reached the same conclusion, highlighting the Syriac elements in the Armenian text of Paul's letters in the commentaries.[5] Since then, however, not much has been published about these commentaries. Needless to say, not much has been discussed in the recent scholarly forums concerning the commentary attributed to St. Ephrem on the apocryphal third letter of St Paul to the Corinthians.

This paper offers preliminary observations of the manuscripts and text of the Armenian version of the commentary on 3 Cor, highlighting certain aspects of its contents and theology in an effort to contribute to the scholarly discussion of their authorship and origin.

Published Texts and Manuscript Evidence

In 1836, the Mekhitharist fathers in San Lazzaro, Venice, published the Armenian commentaries on the books of the Bible attributed to Saint Ephrem.[6] This text was published in four volumes, which included commentaries on the books of the Old Testament and the New Testament, as well as prayers and reflections attributed to Ephrem. Volume Three of this work includes Ephrem's commentaries on the letters of Paul.[7] The commentary on the apocryphal 3 Cor is found on pages 116-123. Almost half a century later, the Mekhitharist fathers published a Latin translation of the same commentary.[8]

In general, the text of Ephrem's commentaries published by the Mekhitharist Fathers is based on a single manuscript in the collection of the Mekhitharist Monastery in Venice. The publisher does not identify the manuscript used to publish the edition. However, comparing a description of the manuscript in the introduction of the book with the colophons of the various Armenian manuscripts in the Mekhitharist Monastery in Venice, helps us identify it as MS1600—the oldest paper manuscript in the Mekhitharist collection.[9] This manuscript, copied in AD 999, includes commentaries on the letters of Paul by Ephrem followed by commentaries on the same letters by John Chrysostom.

A preliminary examination of Armenian manuscript catalogues in several collections worldwide, has identified thirty-one manuscripts of Ephrem's commentaries.[10] These manuscripts contain commentaries either on all the letters or on several of the letters of Paul. Some of the manuscripts contain the Book of Reasons or of Rationale, (Գիրք պատճառաց, *girk' patčaṙac'*), attributed to the thirteenth century Gregory son of Abas, which incorporates the commentary on the letters of Paul. The commentary can also be found intertwined with commentaries by other Church fathers and commentators such as John Chrysostom, Euthalius, Cyril of Jerusalem and Origen.

All thirty-one manuscripts, including one exclusively (Matendaran 5443), contain Ephrem's commentary on Hebrews. This commentary is always inserted after his commentary on 2 Thes and before 1 Tim, thus indicating the location of this letter in the canon of the Pauline corpus of the author of the commentaries. Furthermore, all thirty-one manuscripts lack the commentary on Philemon. The Mekhitharist publisher of the Armenian commentaries offers a plausible explanation for the absence of a commentary on Philemon, attributing it to the plainness and simplicity of the short letter's contents.[11]

The commentaries in question are usually part of a miscellany, a collection of several documents in one manuscript, which in many cases includes John Chrysostom's commentaries and sometimes reflections by other Church fathers. The titles of the commentaries in all the manuscripts identify the author of the commentary as "St. Ephrem the Syrian." In some manuscripts the commentaries bear the title "Commentary on the Fourteen Letters of Paul." Since the collection does not include the letter to Philemon, the fourteenth letter in the list is usually *Third Corinthians*, which appears after 2 Cor and before Gal. The existence of 3 Cor in Ephrem's commentaries indicates the inclusion of this pseudepigraphon in the New Testament canon of the Syrian church during the fourth century.[12] This is further attested by references to 3 Cor in the other writings of Ephrem.[13] Thus, the list and sequence of the letters in almost all complete manuscripts of the commentaries of St. Ephrem are as follows: Rom, 1 Cor, 2 Cor, 3 Cor, Gal, Eph, Philip, Col, 1 Thes, 2 Thes, Heb, 1 Tim, 2 Tim and Titus.

The following are the manuscripts which I was able to locate in the various depositories around the world, which contain the commentaries on the letters of Paul attributed to St Ephram:

V1600:[14]
450 folios, 15X24, Bolorgir. Old number 953 dated to 999AD. This is the oldest paper manuscript in the Mekhitharist collection in Venice. It contains the commentaries on the letters of St. Paul by Ephrem and john Chrysostom. Folios 1-157b contain Ephrem's commentaries on the letters of Paul, excluding Philemon. It includes the commentary on 3 Cor which comes immediately after 2 Cor and before Gal on folios 65b-70b. This is followed by the commentaries attributed to John Chrysostom, on folios 165a-442a.

V1604:[15]
317 folios, 17X26.5, Bolorgir mixed with Yerkadagir. Old number 420 dated to 11th-12th century. Copied by two scribes. The second scribes copied folios 158-240. This manuscript contains the commentaries on the letters of St. Paul by Ephrem intermingled with those of John Chrysostom. Folios 8a-66b contain Ephrem's commentary on the letter to Romans, followed by "Reasons for First Corinthians" on folio 66b. The "Reasons for Ephesians" attributed to Ephrem is on folio 258, while "Reasons for Philippians" on folio 289.

V1609:[16]
412 folios, 17X23.5, Bolorgir. Old number 111 dated to 1608. It contains the commentaries on the letters of St. Paul by Ephrem intermingled with those of John Chrysostom. It includes the commentary on 3 Cor attributed to St. Ephrem which comes immediately after the saint's commentary on 2 Cor and before Gal on folios 175b-180a.

V1612:[17]
809 folios, 15.5X21.2, Bolorgir. Old number 1514 dated to 1719. The contents of this manuscript carefully follow those of the previous manuscript (V1609). It includes the commentary on 3 Cor on folios 304-311, which comes after the commentary on 2 Cor and before the one on Gal.

V1614:[18]

335 folios, 14X19.5, Notr Manr. Old number 436 dated to 18th century. It contains the commentaries on the letters of St. Paul by Ephrem following an introductory section, folios 2a-54b. St. Ephrem's commentaries end on folio 319b and is followed by a commentary on the letter to Philemon attributed to john Chrysostom. This manuscript includes the commentary on 3 Cor attributed to St. Ephrem which comes immediately after the saint's commentary on 2 Cor and before Gal on folios 152a-56b.

St. James, Jerusalem, MSS
J234:[19]

588 folios, 28X20, Bolorgir. Dated to 1603. This manuscript if a collection of commentaries on the Letters of Paul attributed to Anania of Sanahin. It includes commentaries mainly by Ephrem and John Chrysostom, but also of others including Origen. It includes Ephrem's commentary on 3 Cor on folios 242-247a.

J1284:[20]

576 folios, 18X13, different styles of writing, 15th century. This manuscript contains a collection of commentaries on the books of the Old Testament and New Testament including the letters of Paul. The commentary on the Letters of Paul is attributed to Yovhannes Worotnetsi, but in fact is a catena of commentaries attributed to Ephrem and John Chrysostom. It includes Ephrem's commentary on 3 Cor on folios 357a-364a.

Antelias, Lebanon,
A26:[21]

194 folios, 21.8X15.5, Notrgir. Dated to 1673. This manuscript includes commentaries on the Letters of Paul attributed to St. Ephrem and John Chrysostom. It includes the commentary on 3 Cor attributed to St. Ephrem on folios 84a-86a.

A61:[22]

252 folios, 20X14, Notrgir. Dated to the 17th century. This is a miscellany. Among a variety of documents copied in this manuscripts are also the commentaries on the Letters of Paul. It includes commentaries on all the letters of Paul attributed to John Chrysostom and Ephrem. Ephrem's commentary on 3 Cor is copied on folios 102a-106a.

Matenadaran, Armenia, MSS
M57

320 folios, 13.7X9, Bolorgir, dated to 15th century. This is a miscellany that contains, among other documents, the Book of Reasons which contains mainly commentaries on the Books of the Bible by St. Ephrem and St John Chrysostom. Folios 253a-257a includes S.t Ephrem's commentary on 3 Cor.[23]

M190

408 folios, 26.1X15.5, Bolorgir, dated to 1659. This is a complete Bible which contains also the apocryphal 3 Cor, the Sailings of the Apostle Paul and the Rest of the Evangelist John, inserted at the end of the New Testament canon with the Book of Revelation. Folios 397a-398a includes St. Ephrem's commentary on 3 Cor.[24]

M1320

397 folios, 34X25, Bolorgir, dated to 1211. This manuscript contains commentaries on the 14 letters of the Apostle Paul, which includes also the apocryphal 3 Cor. Folios 163b-167b includes St. Ephrem's commentary on 3 Cor.

M1879

383 folios, 23.9 X 17.4, Bolorgir. This 13th-century manuscript is a copy of the Book of Reasons for Gregory the Son of Abbas. Folios 333a-335a includ St. Ephrem's commentary on 3 Cor.

Based on the above, one can easily classify the transmission of the Classical Armenian text of Ephrem's Commentary on 3 Cor through four categories of manuscripts. The most common is commentaries on the Bible, which contain also commentaries on the Letters of Paul including 3 Cor. Another group is of manuscripts containing commentaries on the Letters of Paul including 3 Cor. Several manuscripts contain the Book of Reasons, which is a combination of an Introduction to the Bible and patristic commentaries, which include St. Ephrem's commentary on 3 Cor as "the reasons for St Paul's Third Letter to the Corinthians." Finally, the fourth group is of miscellanies which contain various writings among which the commentary on 3 Cor is inserted.

I am currently working on the Classical Armenian manuscripts of Ephrem's commentary on 3 Cor to prepare its critical text and its English translation with footnotes indicating the variant readings. At the initial stages of the textual work, no serious variations were found in the texts of the four groups of the manuscripts. The English translation of the text of St. Ephrem's commentary in this article is mine based on the Classical Armenian text published by the Mekhitharist fathers.[25]

Ephrem's Text of 3 Cor

As indicated earlier, scholars have demonstrated that the Armenian version of the commentary is a translation from a Syriac original.

Therefore, the text of 3 Cor used by the author must have been a Syriac version or an edition approved by the Syrian Church of the author. This highlights one of the important reasons for studying this commentary in that it preserves a version of 3 Cor that was used by the community of the author of the commentary. Comparing the text of 3 Cor contained in St. Ephrem's commentary to the Greek text (Bodmer Papyrus X) as well as those in the Armenian, Coptic (Heidelberg Papyrus), and Latin manuscripts one can find several unique characteristics in Ephrem's version.[26] As we will demonstrate below, in some instances it is very difficult to conclude whether the specific variation in text indicates a unique reading of 3 Cor preserved in the author's version of 3 Cor, or whether it is because of the author's comment which are interweaved in the text.

Before immersing into the textual variations between Ephrem's 3 Cor and those of the Armenian, Coptic, Greek and Latin version, it is important to state that 3 Cor was considered a canonical book of the New Testament of the author of the commentary. In the commentary, he identifies the heresy targeted in 3 Cor as the false doctrine taught by the Bardaisanians. The author adds, "It is because of this that Bardaisanians did not allow this letter to be part of their apostolic epistles." This comment clearly indicates that for the author of the commentary and for his community, 3 Cor was part of the canon of the New Testament of his time. It also points to the fact that the author was aware of recent collections of the letters of Paul, contemporary to the time of the author, from which 3 Cor was removed by certain heretical movements. In fact, other writings of St. Ephrem and other Syrian Church fathers attest to the fact that 3 Cor was included in their canon of the New Testament.[27]

The contents of St. Ephrem's commentary on 3 Cor can be classified into four sections: 1) an introduction to 3 Cor; 2) the Corinthians' letter to St Paul, 3) the delivery of the Corinthians' letter to Paul; and 4) the Apostle's reply to the Corinthians. Section 1 of the commentary is an introduction to 3 Cor by St. Ephrem. It describes the situation in Corinth and what caused the Corinthians to write to Paul and seek his help:

> Foreign schismatics from yonder, which were born from within themselves, quickly spread among the Corinthians, who were united based on the letters of the Apostle, and divided them. And, because of the evil jealousy which was growing stronger among them, they openly and boldly preached the

heresy of their deceit in public, and did not hide or cover up from all or cover up whatever appeared to be theirs. Meanwhile the elders of the Corinthians, having seen that they were spreading and increasing their preaching, hastened to write to the Apostle in order to show him what they were preaching, so that either he personally would immediately come, or that the refutation and dismissal of their words might be sent from him with great care. Thus concerning these, and whatever is similar to these, they wrote the letter and gave it to be delivered to Paul quickly by the hand of two deacons, saying the following.[28]

A quick glance at the main components of this section makes us conclude that it is not the author's commentary on Section I of the text of 3 Cor.[29] This section, which is found only in the Coptic Heidelberg Papyrus, contains clearly identifiable units which are not found in Ephrem's paragraph quoted above. Section I of 3 Cor reads:

For the Corinthians were in great trouble concerning Paul, that he would depart outr of the world, before it was time. For there were certain men come from Corinth, Simon and Cleobius, saying that there is no resurrection of the flesh, but that of the spirit only, and the human body is not the creation of God, and also concerning the world, that God did not create it, and that God does not know the world, and that Jeuss Christ was not actually crucified, but was only apparently crucified, and that he was not born of Mary, not of the seed of David. And in short, there were many things that they had taught in Corinth, deceiving many others and deciving also themselves. When therefore the Corinthians heard that Paul was at Philippi, they sent a letter to Paul in Macedonia by Threptus and Eutychus the deacons.[30]

Comparing the two paragraphs one notices the missing of all the main component of Section I of 3 Cor from the introductory paragraph by Ephrem. There we read about the Corinthians' concern for St Paul, a listing of the various false teachings of the heretics in Corinth, the identity of the heretics and the names of the two deacons who took the letter to the Apostle. None of these units are found in Ephrem's section 1. We conclude, therefore, that Ephrem's 3 Cor did not include Section 1 and that the introductory paragraph in the commentary is Ephrem's creation.

A slightly different situation is encountered with Section II of 3 Cor, where a brief notice describes the delivery of the letter to Paul. This 5-verse text in 3 Cor is expanded to a two-paragraph narrative in Ephrem's commentary on 3 Cor. While these two paragraphs do not have the identical wording of the text in Section II of 3 Cor, they clearly form a commentary on the section. They contain all the main components of Section II in 3 Cor, except for the names of the deacons who delivered the letters to Paul. St. Ephrem's commentary reads:

> They took the letter and delivered it to the city of Philippi. They were afraid to come to Paul because it happened to be the day of torturing Paul. They tormented him with sticks, and put him in jail, because he has delivered the evil spirit from the girl, who was a magician. And they gave the letter to be delivered by the wife of Apilaphan. However, this was the same night when there was a quake, and the gates of the prison were plainly opened, and his shackles were released. And the prison master freed him from the prison and took him to his house, where the letter was delivered to him.
>
> And as he received the letter, he forgot his shackles, and mourned for the words that he heard. He thus said weeping, it would have been better that I was dead and with the Lord, in hope and peace, and not in the patience of being in shackles for people. Once again the priests of Satan cry out and confuse the people whom I had converted, and lead them astray. And thus, in much agony and persecution and in deceits that Paul was enduring, he prepared a reply to the letter of the Corinthians crying, telling them as follow.

The two paragraphs start with a statement announcing the delivery of the letter to Paul, without mentioning the names of those delivering the letter. This is followed by an elaboration on the Apostle's torture and imprisonment at the time of the delivery of the letter. We read about the reason for Paul's imprisonment which, according to Ephrem, was because he has delivered the evil spirit from the girl, who was a magician. We then read about Paul's reaction as he reads the Corinthians' letter who said weeping, "it would have been better that I was dead and with the Lord." The two paragraphs end with the phrase introducing Paul's letter. All the elements making up the two paragraphs mentioned above are found in Section II of 3 Cor:

> The deacons Threptus and Eutyches brought the letter unto Philippi, so that Paul received it, being in bonds because of Stratonice the wife of Apollophanes, And he forgot his bonds, and was sore afflicted, and cried out, saying: It were better for me to die and to be with the Lord, than to continue in the flesh and to hear such things and the calamities of false doctrine, so that trouble cometh upon trouble. And over and above this so great affliction I am in bonds and behold these evils whereby the devices of Satan are accomplished. Paul therefore, in great affliction, wrote a letter, answering thus.

Comparing the two versions, one can easily observe that St. Ephrem's version is more elaborate. The added elements are biblical and are borrowed from Acts 16. Most probably therefore Ephrem's Section 2 does not reflect another version of 3 Cor. Rather it is the Saint's comments added to the text of Section II.

Continuing our comparison of the texts of 3 Cor in St. Ephrem's commentary with those in the Greek, Armenian, Coptic and Latin manuscripts, one can clearly demonstrate that the text in Ephrem follows that of the Greek Bodmer Papyrus very closely, with a few exceptions. At the beginning of the Corinthians' letter to Paul, all the versions mention the names of the four elders of the Corinthian community in addition to Stephanas. Ephrem's version is the only one which does not mention any of the names of the elders except for Stephanus. There is no reason to assume that the author has intentionally removed the names of the elders. In fact, Even the parts of the text of 3 Cor which he does not comment on, the author usually copies them in his commentary.

Another key variation from the text of 3 Cor in the Greek version is found in the section of St Paul's reply to the Corinthians where he discusses the birth of Jesus. St. Ephrem's version reads:

> That our Jesus Christ was born of Mary and not of being with another man, from the lineage of David, and not because of Joseph's being with her.

This version includes clear insertions that are not found in the Greek version of 3 Cor which reads:

> Christ Jesus was born of Mary from the seed of david by the Holy Spirit sent from heaven by the Father into her.

Ephrem's version is the only one that inserts the explanatory phrases starting with the negating adverb "not." There are two insertions which elaborate on the two of the three statements making up this paragraph. The phrase "not of being with another man" obviously is to elaborate on the meaning of "Christ was born of Mary." The second insertion, "and not of Joseph being with her" is to emphasize that Jesus' Davidic ancestry can be traced through Mary as well. This is a clear example of an exegetical style very common to Ephrem where he inserts his own comments in the text of the book commented on, and interlaces the two together.

General Observations on Style and Theology

Due to the fact that no manuscript containing the original Syriac text of St. Ephrem's commentaries on the Letters of Paul has survived, it is impossible to conclude, by comparison, how authentic the Armenian version of the commentary is to its parent text or the original. Until the discovery of the Syriac original version, one can search the Armenian commentary on 3 Cor for well documented Ephraemic hermeneutics and exegetical and literary styles,[31] demonstrated by scholarly research. This can support the argument that the Armenian version was based on an original written by the Saint himself or at least by his disciples or a school imitating his style.

One of the main characteristics of Ephrem's writings, as in his hymns and commentary on the Diatessaron, is his display of great freedom in what he chooses to comment on.[32] This practice can easily be detected in the commentaries on the letters of Paul. Sometimes the author quotes a paragraph or more of the letter verbatim with a brief comment or no comment at all. At other times he focuses on one word or phrase and offers a lengthy reflection on it. Similar cases are found in the Saint's commentary on 3 Cor. In his comments on St Paul's reply to the Corinthians the author goes over almost three paragraphs with very brief comments. However, when he reaches the phrase "Prince of lawlessness?" he pauses to offers almost a paragraph long of commentary on this, otherwise, biblical phrase (2 Thess 2:8). St. Ephrem elaborates on this phrase saying:

> And he was called Prince because he had authority over armies of his residents. And "lawless" as he called himself, because he did not count his authority over demons big enough, and wanted to become divine over human beings as well. And he slaughtered the prophets, not himself but his prophets. For through Jezebel, Ahab and the kings who were like them he killed the prophets, so that they may not preach the truth, and may open the eyes of those who were calling those made of wood and stone and other matter gods without knowing.[33]

Another example of freedom in choosing what to comment on is found in the author's elaboration on God's saving act in sending the prophets to the house of Israel. In his reply to the Corinthians, referring to God, Paul saying:

> For he was willing to save the house of Isral, therefore distributing from the spirit of Christ, he sent it to the prophets who proclaimed the unerring worship for many times.[34]

Going through this paragraph without comments, the author chooses to dwell on what seems to be a simple phrase, such as "long time":

> So that the same Spirit that preached through the apostles may also preach about faultless worship and the birth of Christ, for many times. That is, for one thousand four hundred and thirty years, from the coming out of the land of Egypt until the arrival of our Lord. The [time] is more or less this much.

The interweaving of his personal comments with the text of the biblical book on which he is commenting is another characteristic of St. Ephrem's writing style frequently found in his commentary on 3 Cor. Usually it is easy to distinguish the Saint's comment from the biblical text. Sometimes, however, it becomes so difficult to distinguish the biblical text from his inserted comments that one needs to decide whether the inserted words in the text represent Ephrem's personal comments or are variations of the biblical text.

As an example of an obvious insertion of Ephrem's comments in the text, we refer to the Saint's comments on the first paragraph of St Paul's reply to the Corinthians in 3 Cor where inserting the phrase "that is to say: he elaborates on certain words and phrases in the paragraph:

> Paul, the prisoner of Jesus Christ, that is to say for the sake of Jesus Christ, to the brothers in Corinth. Greetings in the midst of the great suffering which I have, and in the torture and shackles of the evil's repute. I am surprised as much as I can be, that is to say, I am extremely surprised, that the teachings of the evil one are quickly gaining popularity in the world. Our Lord Jesus Christ will hasten His coming, because of the fact that they disrespect Him by the following: they falsify His words of truth. However, I from the beginning, that is to say after having seen you, taught you what I received from the apostles....

The phrase "that is to say" is found several other times in his commentary on 3 Cor.

Another example of an insertion of a comment in the text is found in the Saint's elaboration on the name Theonoe mentioned by the Corinthians at the beginning of their letter to Paul in 3 Cor 1:8:

We believe in the Lord, as it was revealed to Theonoe, that Christ has delivered you out of the hand of the lawless one, and sent you to us, or you write a letter to us. This [i.e. Theonoe] perhaps is the name of the judge who shackled him and put him in prison in the city of the Philippians.

Meanwhile, the actual text of this paragraph reads:

For we believe as it was revealed to Theonoe that the Lord has delivered you out of the hand of the lawless one.[35]

There is no doubt in this example that the elaboration on the word Theonoe as "perhaps the name of the judge who shackled him and put him in prison in the city of the Philippians" is an insertion by St. Ephrem himself. On the other hand, St. Ephrem's comment on an earlier part of the same paragraph leaves the reader with the challenge to decide whether the variation in the text is a result of the insertion of his own comments, or a consequence of the Saint's use of a different version of 3 Cor. The beginning of his commentary on the Corinthian's letter to Paul in 3 Cor starts with the following:

Stephanus and the elders who are with him, to Paul, brother in the Lord, greeting. Two men have come to Corinth, Simon and Cleobius and are converting many faithful to them. But not with words of the truth do they convert, rather with corrupted words, to which you only should respond.

The subtle insertion of his comments among the Biblical verses can be best demonstrated by quoting the English translation of the same paraqgraph in the text of 3 Cor, which reads:

Stephanus and the presbyters who are with him, Daphnus, Eubulus, Theophilus and Xenon, to Paul their brother in the Lord, greeting. Two men have come to Corinth, Simon and Cleobius, who pervert the faith of many through pernicious words we want you to respond to.

In addition to the exclusion of the names of the elders, the adjective "pernicious" defining the words of the false preachers has been expanded in Ephrem's commentary to the phrase: "not with words of the truth do they convert, rather with corrupted words." The reader is left to decide whether this phrase existed in St. Ephrem's version of 3 Cor or whether it is his elaboration on the adjective. To the best of my knowledge no version that I have come across includes this elaboration on the nature of the words used by the false preachers. Consequently, it is fair to conclude that these are the words of the commentator.

Another key feature in St. Ephrem's writings is his focus on specific dangers threatening the Christian community of Ephrem's time.[36] The threats discussed by Ephrem in his writings usually arose mainly from the influence of the teachings of heretics such as Marcion, Bardaisan and Mani on the fourth-century Syrian Church.[37] Obviously, they could not have existed at the time of St Paul's writing of his letters. However, the Saint feels free to refer to them to elaborate on the meaning of the biblical text at hand. Similar approaches are found in the commentary on 3 Cor. According to the commentator the main purpose of writing this letter was to refute the 'doctrine of the teachers from the house of Bardaisan.'[38] In fact as mentioned earlier, and typical of the Saint's commentary style, he spends a paragraph elaborating on this point:

This is the doctrine of the teachers of the house of Bardaisan. It is because of this that Bardaisanians did not allow this letter to be part of their apostolic epistles. In the Book of Acts the following is said by the Apostle: "After me, when I am gone, there will enter among you ravening wolves who will not spare the disciples. Wicked men will rise among you who will convert disciples to follow them." Thus from the days of the Apostle, and as the Apostle himself prophesied, and as the Corinthians wrote, this cult was established. For the disciples of Bardaisan believe that they learned this from the teacher Bardaisan, and from him they wrote even the *praxautos*. For among the miracles and signs written about the Apostles, they write lawlessness about the Apostles, discrediting the Apostles anew. It is because of this that they say, "about which we wrote to you in a letter. Hasten personally and come to aid us, you in person. So that through your vision and words this city of Corinth may remain without lure, and their stupidity may be made known to all and be openly rejected by all through your truth and preaching".

Furthermore, direct and indirect quotations from, or references and allusions to stories or events in, the Old Testament are frequently used by St. Ephrem in his writings to support his argument and to elaborate on his point of view. In fact at times, Ephrem intertwines these Old Testament stories by way of allusion rather than by direct quote.[39] Elaborating on the meaning of "long time" that 3 Cor indicates it took the Holy Spirit to preach through the Old Testament prophets, St. Ephrem elaborates referring to the Old Testament:

This, the same Spirit that preached through the Apostles preached also through the prophets for a long time the unerring worship of God and the birth of Christ. That is to say, one thousand four hundred and thirty years.

This is more or less the time from the exodus of the land of the Egyptians to the coming of Christ.

Explaining how the "Lawless Prince" of 3 Cor fought God and opposed God's redemptive plan for us by using Satan's agents on earth: the Old Testament persecutors of the people of God, e.g. Jezebel, Ahab and others, St. Ephrem adds:

And he slaughtetred the prophets, not himself but his prophets. For through Jezebel, Ahab and the kings who were like them he killed the prophets, so that they may not preach the truth and may open the eyes of those who were ignorantly calling the things made of wood and stone and other matter 'gods'.

Moreover, in his reference to those heretics who had "the faith of the serpent" he elaborates on the phrase "the faith of the serpent" referring to the Old Testament story of Adam and Eve, as follows:

They Have the faith of the cursed serpent. That is to say the judgment which came because of the cursed serpent: 'earth you were and to earth you shall return.' They certainly had this. For they believed like the serpent did, that the house of Adam will remain forever on earth.

Conclusion

The existence of the commentary on 3 Cor attributed to St. Ephrem exclusively in Classical Armenian manuscript restricted the accessibility of western scholars to this important document. It is because of this that not much has been said about the commentaries in general and the one on 3 Cor specifically. This highlights the need for a critical translation of the Classical Armenian text into English.

The existence of the commentary confirms that the apocryphal 3 Cor was considered canonical and authentic Pauline by the author of the commentary who places it after his commentary on 2 Cor and before the one on Galatians. Not only does this writing refer to the author of 3 Cor as Paul and the Apostle, it even explains its text against the background of the life and ministry of the Apostle.

Scholars have demonstrated that the Classical Armenian text is a translation of a Syriac original. Based on our preliminary examination of the contents of the commentary on 3 Cor and the style of commenting on the text, one can easily conclude that the commentary is in line with the theology and style of the fourth century Syrian Saint Ephrem.

The commentary could very well have been authored by the Saint himself. If not, it could be a pseudepigraphon by one of his disciples or a member of the Ephraemic school.

Notes

Introduction

[1] Alternate spellings of "Antiochian" or "Antiochene" are not uniformly applied in the literature, but refer to the same tradition nevertheless. I am following "Antiochian" here to accommodate the title of the volume of this book.

[2] Brevard Childs, *The Struggle to Understand Isaiah as Christian Scripture* (Grand Rapids: Eerdmans Publishing Company, 2004), p. 130. The article he refers to is Bradley Nassif, "The 'Spiritual Exegesis' of Scripture: The School of Antioch Revisited," *Anglican Theological Review* (Vol. LXXV: 4, 1993).

[3] 'Spiritual Exegesis' in the School of Antioch," Bradley Nassif in *New Perspectives on Historical Theology: Essays in Memory of John Meyendorff*, Foreword by Henry Chadwick, Edited by Bradley Nassif (Grand Rapids, MI: Eerdmans, 1996), 344-377. The article extensively examines the contributions of only nine authorities who have written on this subject over the past century, and critiques the secondary literature in which the subject appears.

[4] Bradley Nassif, "Antiochene Θεωρία in John Chrysostom's Exegesis" in *The Bible in the Eastern and Oriental Orthodox Churches*" ed. Vahan Hovanhessian (New York, New York: Peter Lang Publishers, 2009).

[5] Donald Fairbairn, *Grace and Christology in the Early Church* (New York, New York: Oxford University Press, 2003).

[6] For example, S. Hidal, "Exegesis of the Old Testament in the Antiochene School with its Prevalent Literal and Historical Method," in *Hebrew Bible/Old Testament: A History of Its Interpretation*, vol. 1/1 (Gottengen: Vandenhoeck & Ruprecht, 1996), 543-568; A. M. Schor, "Theodoret on the 'School of Antioch': A Network Approach," Journal of Early Christian Studies 15 (Dec. 9, 2007): 517-562; C. Kennengiesser, "Biblical Exegesis and Hermeneutics in Syria," *Handbook of Patristic Exegesis: The Bible in Ancient Christianity*, vol. 2 (Leiden: Brill), 769-839; 875-877; 885-918; C. Moreschini and E. Norelli, translated by Matthew J. O'Connell, "The Antiochene School," in *Early Christian Greek and Latin Literature: A Literary History* (Peabody, MA: Hendrickson Publishers, 2005).

[7] Robert Wilken, *John Chrysostom and the Jews. Rhetoric and reality in the late 4th Century* (Berkeley-Los Angeles-London: University of California Press, 1983); Wayne Meeks and Robert Wilken, *Jews and Christians in Antioch in the*

First Four Centuries of the Common Era (SBL Sources for Biblical Study 13. Missoula, Montana; Scholars Press for the SBL, 1978).

Exegesis for John Chrysostom

[1] Even Bultmann's own endeavor as a whole is referred to as 'theology." See e.g. Walter Schmithals, *Die Theologie Rudlf Bultmann,* Tübingen 1966, 2.Aufl. 1967.

[2] Even Pierre Teilhard de Chardin with his Point Omega and Noosphere theory is not immune to Hegel's influence.

[3] One can add here a similar passage in Isaiah where the prophet confines to a scroll the teaching that has been refused by the people. It is clear that it is its being written which makes it binding forever: "Bind up the testimony, seal the teaching among my disciples. I will wait for the Lord, who is hiding his face from the house of Jacob, and I will hope in him. Behold, I and the children whom the Lord has given me are signs and portents in Israel from the Lord of hosts, who dwells on Mount Zion. And when they say to you, 'Consult the mediums and the wizards who chirp and mutter,' should not a people consult their God? Should they consult the dead on behalf of the living? To the teaching and to the testimony! Surely for this word which they speak there is no dawn." (Is 8:16-20)

[4] See my "The Book of Jeremiah and the Pentateuchal Torah" in Theodore G. Stylianopoulos, ed., *Sacred Text and Interpretation,* Holy Cross Orthodox Press, Brookline, Massachusetts, 2006, pp.7-36.

[5] The same applies to the church of Corinth. Imagining that the tradition of the Eucharist is to be found in the way it was celebrated at Corinth before Paul corrected it would make out of it a 'demoniac celebration' worthy of divine condemnation: "When you meet together, it is *not* the Lord's supper that you eat." (1 Cor 11:20)

[6] Homily I on the Gospel of St. Matthew in P. Schaff, ed., *The Nicene and Post-Nicene Fathers* (Grand Rapids, 1st Series, x 1978).

[7] See e.g. Deut 5:1; 6:3; 26:16; 28:13.

[8] This in turn explains why the only debate in which he is seriously referred to is the pelagian/semipelagian one, which deals with the "deeds" of "grace."

[9] *On the Priesthood,* 4.5. From *Nicene and Post-Nicene Fathers,* First Series, Vol. 9. Edited by Philip Schaff. Buffalo, NY: Christian Literature Publishing Co., 1889.

[10] *Functional and Dysfunctional Christianity,* Holy Cross Orthodox Press, Brookline, Massachusetts, 1998, pp.4-5.

[11] "There was... a certain presbyter named John, a man of noble birth and of exemplary life, and possessed of such wonderful powers of eloquence and persuasion that he was declared by the sophist, Libanius the Syrian, to surpass all the orators of the age. When this sophist was on his death-bed he was asked by his friends who should take his place. 'It would have been John,' replied he,

'had not the Christians taken him from us.'" (Sozomen, *Ecclesiastical History*, 8.2 (translation *The Nicene and Post-Nicene Fathers*).

[12] Chrysostom then proceeds to speak of the similar setting of Dan 7:9-11.

[13] Duane A. Garrett, *An Analysis of the Hermeneutics of John Chrysostom's Commentary on Isaiah 1-8 With An English Translation.* The Edwin Mellen Press, 1992, pp.123-5.

[14] See also Jesus' answer "You know the commandments" to the man inquiring of him as to what "do to inherit eternal life" (Mk 10:17-19; Lk 18:18-20).

[15] Mt 7:1-23; 25:1-46.

[16] Deut 4:9

[17] As the catecheses Cyril of Jerusalem—another bishop of the Roman province Syria—were meant to do.

[18] Some translations have "Word," understanding that Chrysostom was referring to the word of Scripture or the word of the gospel. There is no doubt that he was intending to say that the minister is to administer, through his own word[s], the word[s] of God. Indeed, earlier Chrysostom alludes to Ephesians when he writes: "For the Church of Christ, according to Saint Paul, is Christ's body, and he who is entrusted with its care ought to train it up to a state of healthiness, and beauty unspeakable, and to look everywhere, lest any spot or wrinkle, or other like blemish should mar its vigor and comeliness." This is directly taken from Ephesians 5 where Paul states clearly that this action of cleansing care of Christ's body is done "by the washing of water with the word" (v.26). In Ephesians the "word" refers to the word of God (6:17) or the gospel (1:13).

[19] *On the Priesthood,* 4.2,3.

[20] Due to the Ptolemaic Royal Library that came under Roman imperial auspices.

[21] Time and again at Oriental-Orthodox international symposia it was stated that the difference was merely formal and not material.

Biblical Fragments from the Christian Library

[1] On these expeditions and the resultant Turfan Collection, see Berlin-Brandenburg Academy of Sciences and Humanities, *Turfan Studies* (Berlin: Berlin-Brandenburg Academy of Sciences and Humanities, 2007); Albert von le Coq, *Buried Treasures of Chinese Turkestan* (trans. Anna Barwell; London: George Allen and Unwin Ltd., 1928) and Mary Boyce, *A Catalogue of the Iranian Manuscripts in Manichaean Script in the German Turfan Collection* (*Deutsche Akademie der Wissenschaften zu Berlin, Institut für Orientforschung, Veröffentlichung Nr. 45*), (Berlin: Akademie Verlag, 1960): ix-xxvii.

[2] The project team consists of Dr. Erica C. D. Hunter (project leader), Prof. Nicholas Sims-Williams, Prof. Peter Zieme and the present author. I wish to express my thanks to the other project team members for information and corrections contributed to this article.

[3] Notably two fragments from a Sogdian Psalter with Greek headlines and possibly a letter mentioning Byzantine dignitaries, all described below. Possible

connections between Turfan and Byzantine Christianity are discussed in Werner Sundermann, "Byzanz und Bulayïq," in *Iranian and Indo-European Studies: Memorial Volume of Otakar Klíma* (ed. Petr Vavroušek; Praha: Enigma Corporation, 1994), 255-64.

[4] On the 97 fragments in Syriac from Turfan brought back to St. Petersburg by N. N. Krotkov at the same time as the Prussian Turfan Expeditions were taking place, see E. N. Meshcherskaya, "The Syriac Fragments in the N.N. Krotkov Collection," in *Turfan, Khotan Und Dunhuang* (ed. Ronald E. Emmerick et al.; Berlin: Akademie Verlag, 1996), 221-27. These fragments are currently uncatalogued and unpublished.

[5] On the monastery complex of Bulayïq where most of the Christian materials were found, see Nicholas Sims-Williams, "Bulayïq," *Encyclopaedia Iranica* 4:545. On the initial discovery of Christian manuscripts at Bulayïq, see von le Coq, *Buried Treasures*, 100-01. On the nature of Christianity in Turfan, see Wolfgang Hage, "Das Christentum in Der Turfan-Oase," in *Synkretismus in den Religionen Zentralasiens* (ed. Walther Heissig and Hans-Joachim Klimkeit; Wiesbaden: Otto Harrassowitz, 1987), 46-57 and Nicholas Sims-Williams, "Sogdian and Turkish Christians in the Turfan and Tun-Huang Manuscripts," in *Turfan and Tun-Huang, the Texts: Encounter of Civilizations on the Silk Route* (ed. Alfredo Cadonna; Firenze: Leo S. Olschki Editore, 1992), 43-61.

[6] On Christian materials from Dunhuang, see Nicholas Sims-Williams and James Hamilton, *Documents Turco-Sogdiens du IXe-Xe siècle de Touen-houang* (*Corpus Inscriptorum Iranicarum, Part II, Vol. III*) (London: School of Oriental and African Studies, 1990), 51-61, 63-76 and Wassilios Klein and Jürgen Tubach, "Ein Syrisch-Christliches Fragment aus Dunhuang/China," *ZDMG* 144 (1994): 1-13, 446. On the very few Christian finds from Qara-khoto, see N. Pigoulewsky, "Fragments Syriaques et Syro-turcs de Hara-Hoto et de Tourfan," *ROC* 30 (1935-1936): 3-46 and Peter Zieme, "A Cup of Cold Water," in *Jingjiao: The Church of the East in China and Central Asia* (ed. Roman Malek and Peter Hofrichter; Sankt Augustin: Institut Monumenta Serica, 2006), 341-45.

[7] Sims-Williams, "Sogdian and Turkish Christians," 49, 50-51, 54.

[8] These will all be included in the catalogue of Syriac fragments from Turfan being compiled by Erica C. D. Hunter and the present author. For an earlier overview, see Miklós Maróth, "Die Syrischen Handschriften in der Turfan-Sammlung," in *Ägypten, Vorderasien, Turfan: Probleme der Edition und Bearbeitung Altorientalischer Handschriften* (ed. Horst Klengel and Werner Sundermann; Berlin: Akademie Verlag, 1991), 126-28.

[9] Signature numbers in bold are those currently in use. Those in parentheses are the original numbers recorded by the Turfan expeditions, which are frequently found in the literature. The new signature numbers generally reflect the language or script of the fragments, although each group includes some which have been mislabeled. **M** = Manichaean fragments; **MIK** = Museum für Indische Kunst (former name of the Museum für Asiatische Kunst); **n** = "Nestorian" fragments

[10] (Sogdian in Syriac script); **So** = Sogdian script fragments; **SyrHT** = Syriac fragments; **U** = Uyghur fragments (in Uyghur or Syriac script).

[10] The Hudra is the main liturgical text of the Church of the East, containing the cycle of services for the whole liturgical year.

[11] Eduard Sachau, "Litteratur-Bruchstücke aus Chinesisch-Turkistan," *SPAW* (1905): 967-70, translated in P. Y. Saeki, *The Nestorian Documents and Relics in China*, 2nd ed. (Tokyo: Maruzen Company Ltd, 1951), 340-43.

[12] Folios 1-5 translated in Hieronymus Engberding, "Fünf Blätter eines Alten Ostsyrischen Bitt- Und Bußgottesdienstes Aus Innerasien," *OstStud* 14 (1965): 121-48. Folios 20v-21r edited in Sachau, "Litteratur-Bruchstücke," 970-73 and translated in Saeki, *Nestorian Documents*, 343-47.

[13] F. W. K. Müller and W. Lentz, "Sogdische Texte II," *SPAW* (1934): 559-64. Merv was an important centre in Sassanid Persia's eastern province of Margiana (modern-day Turkmenistan).

[14] Miklós Maróth, "Ein Fragment eines Syrischen Pharmazeutischen Rezeptbuches," *AoF* 11 (1984): 115-25.

[15] Miklós Maróth, "Ein Brief aus Turfan," *AoF* 12 (1985): 283-87.

[16] Miklós Maróth, "Eine Unbekannte Version der Georgios-Legende aus Turfan," *AoF* 18 (1991): 86-108. To these fragments published by Maróth can be added **SyrHT 381** (T II B 53 No. 8), not included in his publication.

[17] To be published soon by Miklós Maróth.

[18] J. P. Asmussen, "The Sogdian and Uighur-Turkish Christian Literature in Central Asia before the Real Rise of Islam: A Survey," in *Indological and Buddhist Studies: Volume in Honour of Professor J. W. De Jong on His Sixtieth Birthday* (ed. L. A. Hercus et al.; Canberra: Faculty of Asian Studies, 1982), 11-29; Nicholas Sims-Williams, "Die Christlich-Sogdischen Handschriften von Bulayïq," in *Ägypten, Vorderasien, Turfan* (ed. Horst Klengel and Werner Sundermann; Berlin: Akademie Verlag, 1991), 119-25; Nicholas Sims-Williams, "Christianity, IV. Christian Literature in Middle Iranian Languages," *Encyclopaedia Iranica* 5: 534-35; Nicholas Sims-Williams, "Christian Literature in Middle Iranian Languages," in *The Literature of Pre-Islamic Iran* (ed. Ronald E. Emmerick and Maria Macuch. London: I. B. Tauris, 2009), 266-87. On the Christian fragments in Sogdian script, see Christiane Reck, "A Survey of the Christian Sogdian Fragments in Sogdian Script in the Berlin Turfan Collection," in *Controverses des Chrétiens dans l'Iran sassanide* (ed. Christelle Jullien; Paris: Association pour l'Avancement des Études Iraniennes, 2008), 191-205.

[19] All Christian materials from Turfan in either Sogdian or New Persian in Syriac script will be included in a catalogue being compiled by Nicholas Sims-Williams as part of *The Christian Library at Turfan* Project (hereafter referred to as Sims-Williams, *Catalogue*). Christian fragments in Sogdian script will be catalogued by Christiane Reck in *Mitteliranische Handschriften*, Teil 3, a forthcoming volume of the cataloguing project of the Akademie der Wissenschaften zu Göttingen.

[20] Olaf Hansen, "Berliner Soghdische Texte I: Bruchstücke einer Soghdischen Version der Georgspassion (C1)," *APAW* 10 (1941): 1-38; Ilya Gershevitch, "On

the Sogdian St. George Passion," *JRAS* (1946): 179-84; E. Benveniste, "Fragments des Actes de Saint Georges en version sogdienne," *JA* 234 (1943-1945): 91-116.

[21] Edited initially in Olaf Hansen, "Berliner Soghdische Texte II: Bruchstücke Der Großen Sammelhandschrift C2," *AWLMJ* (1955): 821-918 and subsequently with major corrections in Nicholas Sims-Williams, *The Christian Sogdian Manuscript C2* (*Berliner Turfantexte XII*), (Berlin: Akademie Verlag, 1985). For specific parts of this manuscript, see also Nicholas Sims-Williams, "A Sogdian Fragment of a Work of Dadišoʻ Qatraya," *AsMaj* 18 (N.S.) (1973): 88-105; Nicholas Sims-Williams, "Syro-Sogdica I: An Anonymous Homily on the Three Periods of the Solitary Life," *OCP* 47 (1981): 441-46; Nicholas Sims-Williams, "Syro-Sogdica II: A Metrical Homily by Bābay Bar Nṣibnāye 'On the Final Evil Hour'," *OCP* 48 (1982): 171-76; Nicholas Sims-Williams, "Traditions Concerning the Fates of the Apostles in Syriac and Sogdian," in *Gnosisforschung und Religionsgeschichte: Festschrift für Kurt Rudolph Zum 65. Geburtstag* (ed. Holger Preißler and Hubert Seiwert; Marburg: Diagonal-Verlag, 1994 [1995]), 287-95.

[22] Martin Schwartz, "A Page of a Sogdian *Liber Vitae*," in *Corolla Iranica: Papers in Honour of Prof. Dr. David Neil Mackenzie on the Occasion of His 65th Birthday on April 8th, 1991* (ed. Ronald E. Emmerick and Dieter Weber; Frankfurt: Peter Lang, 1991), 157-66.

[23] Werner Sundermann, "Der Schüler Fragt den Lehrer: Eine Sammlung Biblischer Rätsel in Soghdischer Sprache," in *A Green Leaf: Papers in Honour of Professor Jes P. Asmussen* (ed. Werner Sundermann, Jacques Duchesne-Guillemin and Faridun Vahman; Leiden: E. J. Brill, 1988), 173-86.

[24] Nicholas Sims-Williams, "A Sogdian Version of the «Gloria in Excelsis Deo»," in *Au Carrefours des Religions: Mélanges offerts à Philippe Gignoux* (ed. Rika Gyselen; Bures-sur-Yvette: Groupe pour l'Étude de la Civilisation du Moyen-Orient, 1995), 257-62.

[25] Nicholas Sims-Williams, "Christian Sogdian Texts from the Nachlass of Olaf Hansen I: Fragments of the Life of Serapion," *BSOAS* 58 (1995): 50-68. Serapion (d. ca. 362) was bishop of Thmuis in Lower Egypt and an important proponent of Nicene Christology.

[26] Werner Sundermann, "Ein Soghdisches Fragment der Mār Eugen-Legende," in *Splitter aus der Gegend von Turfan: Festschrift Für Peter Zieme Anläßlich Seines 60. Geburtstags* (ed. Mehmet Ölmez and Simone-Christiane Raschmann; Istanbul-Berlin: Şafak Matbaacılık, 2002), 309-31. Mar Awgen (Eugenius) was the founder of coenobitic monasticism in Mesopotamia and is highly revered in the Church of the East.

[27] Nicholas Sims-Williams, "A Christian Sogdian Polemic against the Manichaeans," in *Religious Themes and Texts of Pre-Islamic Iran and Central Asia* (ed. Carlo G. Cereti, Mauro Maggi and Elio Provasi. Wiesbaden: Dr. Ludwig Reichert Verlag, 2003), 399-408.

[28] See Asmussen, "Sogdian and Uighur-Turkish Christian Literature," 11-29 and Simone-Christiane Raschmann, "Traces of Christian Communities in the Old

Turkish Documents," in *Studies in Turkic Philology: Festschrift in Honour of the 80th Birthday of Professor Geng Shimin* (ed. Dingjing Zhang and Abdurishid Yakup; Beijing: Minzu University Press, 2009), 408-25. All Uyghur Christian texts will be included in an edition being compiled by Peter Zieme as part of *The Christian Library at Turfan* Project and catalogued by Simone Raschmann in a forthcoming volume of *Alttürkische Handschriften* in the cataloguing project of the Akademie der Wissenschaften zu Göttingen.

[29] Unfortunately, the original manuscript went missing in the aftermath of World War II. The text has been published and translated several times, including F. W. K. Müller, "Uigurica I," *APAW* (1908): 5-10; W. Bang, "Türkische Bruchstücke einer nestorianischen Georgpassion," *Mus* 39 (1926): 43-53; C. E. Малов, *Памятники древнетюркской письменности Монголии И Киргизии.* (Москва-Ленинград: Издателство Академии Наук СССР, 1951), 131-38. See also Kahar Barat, "Old Uyghur Christianity and the Bible," *AmAsRev* 5, No. 2 (1987): 18-22 and Aloïs van Tongerloo, "Ecce Magi ab Oriente Venerunt," in *Philosophie-Philosophy Tolerance* (ed. A. Théodoridès. Brussels: Louvain la Neuve, 1992), 57-74.

[30] Albert von le Coq, "Ein Christliches und ein Manichäisches Manuskriptfragment in Türkischer Sprache aus Turfan (Chinesisch-Turkistan)," *SPAW* (1909): 1205-08; Bang, "Türkische Bruchstücke," 53-64; Anthony Arlotto, "Old Turkic Oracle Books," *MonSer* 29 (1970-71): 693-96.

[31] Albert von le Coq, "Türkische Manichaica aus Chotscho III," *APAW* (1922): 48-49; Bang, "Türkische Bruchstücke," 64-75.

[32] Peter Zieme, "Ein Hochzeitssegen uigurischer Christen," in *Scholia: Beiträge zur Turkologie und Zentralasienkunde* (ed. Klaus Röhrborn and Horst Wilfrid Brands; Wiesbaden: Otto Harrassowitz, 1981), 221-32.

[33] Peter Zieme, "Das nestorianische Glaubensbekenntnis in einem alttürkischen Fragment aus Bulayïq," *UAJ* N.F. 15 (1997/1998): 173-80.

[34] Peter Zieme, "Notes on a Bilingual Prayer Book from Bulayık," in *Hidden Treasures and Intercultural Encounters: Studies on East Syriac Christianity in China and Central Asia* (ed. Dietmar W. Winkler and Li Tang. Wien: LIT Verlag, 2009), 167-80. The present author is concurrently preparing an article on the Syriac portions of this booklet. Other Uyghur Christian fragments are addressed in Peter Zieme, "Zu den Nestorianish-Türkischen Turfantexten," in *Sprache, Geschichte und Kultur der Altaischen Völker: Protokollband Der XII Tagung der Permanent International Altaistic Conference 1969 in Berlin* (ed. Georg Hazai and Peter Zieme. Berlin: Akademie-Verlag, 1974), 661-68 and Peter Zieme, "Zwei Ergänzungen zu der Christlich-Türkischen Handschrift T II B 1," *AoF* 5 (1977): 271-72.

[35] This is discussed in more depth in Sims-Williams, "Sogdian and Turkish Christians." See also Dickens, "Multilingual Christian Manuscripts."

[36] See Jean Dauvillier, "Les Provinces Chaldéennes 'de l'Extérieur' au Moyen Age," in *Mélanges Offerts Au R. P. Ferdinand Cavallera* (Toulouse: Bibliothèque de l'Institut Catholique, 1948), 260-316 and Erica C. D. Hunter, "The Church of the East in Central Asia," *BJRL* 78 (1996): 129-42.

37   We do not know when Christianity first came to Turfan, whether before or after the Uyghurs established their Kingdom there. As noted above, the Christian texts from Turfan are usually dated between the 9th and 13th/14th centuries, although an in-depth study of all the dating indicators, such as palaeography, has yet to be done.

38   Zieme, "Notes on a Bilingual Prayer Book," 172. On other interactions between Christianity, Buddhism and Manichaeism hinted at in the Turfan documents, see Ian Gillman and Hans-Joachim Klimkeit, *Christians in Asia before 1500* (Ann Arbor: University of Michigan Press, 1999), 258-62; Christiane Reck, "Die Bekehrung einer Christin zum manichäischen Glauben? Probleme bei der Interpretation eines fragmentarischen Textes," in *Inkulturation des Christentums im Sasanidenreich* (ed. Arafa Mustafa and Jürgen Tubach; Wiesbaden: Reichert Verlag, 2007), 55-70; Christiane Reck, "Ein Kreuz zum Andenken. Die buddhistischen soghdischen Fragmente der Berliner Turfansammlung," in *Aspects of Research into Central Asian Buddhism: In Memoriam Kōgi Kudara* (ed. Peter Zieme; Turnhout: Brepols, 2008), 277-98.

39   Amongst the Christian fragments are a number that are amuletic or talismanic in nature, including two that can be connected together: **SyrHT 99** (T II B 53 = 1687) and **SyrHT 330** (1863), discussed in Erica C. D. Hunter, "Traversing time and location. A prayer-amulet of Mar Tamsis from Turfan," in *Proceedings of the 3rd International Conference on "Research on the Church of the East in China and Central Asia"* (ed. Dietmar W. Winkler and Li Tang; Wien: LIT Verlag, forthcoming). On **U 328** (T III Kurutka), an Uyghur Christian text that includes incantational material, see Peter Zieme, "Türkische Zuckungsbücher," *Scripta Ottomanica Et Res Altaicae. Festschrift Barbara Kellner-Heinkele* (ed. Ingeborg Hauenschild, Claus Schönig and Peter Zieme; Wiesbaden: Harrassowitz Verlag, 2002), 390. The present author is concurrently preparing an article dealing with a Syriac passage in this text.

40   Sogdian text and German translation: F. W. K. Müller, "Soghdische Texte I," *APAW* 1912 (1913): 84-87. English translation: Gillman and Klimkeit, *Christians in Asia before 1500*, 252-53.

41   Full text in the Hudra [Thoma Darmo, *Ktaba da-Qdam wad-Batar wad-Hudra wad-Kashkol wad-Gazza w-Qala d-'Udrane 'am Ktaba d-Mazmure*, Vol. I (Trichur, Kerala: Church of the East, 1960)] is ܪܘܡܐ ܥܠ ܫܘܥܐ ܪܝܡ.

42   The printed edition of the Hudra has ܐܒܪܗܡ, ܥܡ ܢܪܣܝ ܘܡܪ ܘܒܪ̈ܨܘܡܐ ܗܘ ܛܘܒܢܐ ܚܒܪܐ ܥܡ, "and Mar Narsai and Mar Barsauma the blessed companion, with Abraham."

43   Darmo, *Ktaba da-Qdam wad-Batar*, Vol. I, 446. My thanks to Sebastian Brock for identifying the source of this text in the printed edition of the Hudra.

44   Abbreviated form of the full title: He set my feet upon the rock (Ps. 40:2).

45   Compare translation in Arthur John Maclean, *East Syrian Daily Offices* (London: Rivington, Percival, 1894), 125. As noted above, the printed Hudra text includes Mar Barsauma, "the blessed companion" (of Mar Narsai) between the references to Mar Narsai and Abraham, but this name is not included in

SyrHT 80. Barsauma was the Metropolitan of Nisibis at the time that the School of Nisibis was re-founded in the late 5th century.

[46] On the historical Christology of the Church of the East and the inappropriate use of "Nestorian" to describe the Church, see Sebastian P. Brock, "The Christology of the Church of the East in the Synods of the Fifth to Early Seventh Centuries: Preliminary Considerations and Materials," in *Aksum, Thyateira: A Festschrift for Archbishop Methodios of Thyateira and Great Britain* (ed. George Dion Dragas; London: Editorial Committee, 1985), 125-42 and Sebastian P. Brock, "The 'Nestorian' Church: A Lamentable Misnomer," *BJRL* 78 (1996): 23-35.

[47] My thanks to Mar Awa, bishop of the Assyrian Church of the East in California, and various members of the Hugoye Discussion List (Thomas Carlson, Sergey Minov, Steven Ring, and David Taylor) for assistance in identifying some of the individuals in this passage. On these leaders of the School of Nisibis, see William Wright, *A Short History of Syriac Literature* (London: A. and C. Black, 1894), 33-37, 58-59, 114-115; Arthur Vööbus, *History of the School of Nisibis* (*Corpus Scriptorum Christianorum Orientalium 266/Sub. 26*) (Louvain: Secrétariat du Corpus SCO, 1965), 57-121, 134-222, 278-79; Jean-Maurice Fiey, "Diptyqes nestoriens du XIVe siècle," *AnBoll* 81 (1963): 390-392; Sebastian P. Brock, "The Nestorian Diptychs: A Further Manuscript," *AnBoll* 89 (1971): 182-83.

[48] **SyrHT 337** also contains a reference to ܡܪܝܡ ܐܡܗ ܕܡܫܝܚܐ (*Maryam, ameh d-mashiʰā*), "Mary, the Mother of Christ."

[49] This exact passage is not included in Maclean, *East Syrian Daily Offices*.

[50] My thanks to Sergey Minov for clarifying the identity of some of the individuals in this passage. See also lists in diptychs from the Church of the East discussed in: Fiey, "Diptyqes nestoriens," 394 and Brock, "Nestorian Diptychs," 183.

[51] On the dates of extant Peshitta manuscripts, see Sebastian P. Brock, *The Bible in the Syriac Tradition (Gorgias Handbooks, Vol.* (Piscataway, NJ: Gorgias Press, 2006), 42-47, 49, 122-24. The Turfan fragments thus fall into the *Textus Receptus* stage in the development of the Peshitta text.

[52] Dickens, "Importance of the Psalter."

[53] On which, see Brock, *The Bible*, 18-20, 27-29, 35-37.

[54] See Brock, *The Bible*, 43-44, 114-17.

[55] See Brock, *The Bible*, 142-43.

[56] For a handy table, see Brock, *The Bible*, 138.

[57] ܐ -ܛ = 1-9, ܝ-ܨ = 10-90, ܩ = 100.

[58] As noted above, these (along with examples of Psalmic material from elsewhere in Central Asia) are described in more detail in Dickens, "Importance of the Psalter."

[59] Nicholas Sims-Williams, at the "Christian Manuscripts from Turfan" workshop in Berlin, March 27-28, 2009, plausibly suggested that the compiler began with Psalter "C" in recognition of the previously identified Pahlavi Psalter and Syriac-New Persian Psalter, described below, which were perhaps considered Psalters "A" and "B."

60   Not enough remains to determine if Psalters "H," "L" and "M" originally had headings, canons or prayers.

61   This text will be published by Peter Zieme and the present author.

62   Initially identified by Erica C. D. Hunter as Psalmic material. For a drawing of a Uyghur face with head-dress, see the Uyghur Christian fragment **U 5179** (T II B 62/512), discussed in Peter Zieme, "Zwei Ergänzungen."

63   Continuation of the word begun at the end of l. 4: ܡܠܐܟܘܗܝ, "his angels."

64   See note above on ll. 3-4 of the Syriac text.

65   The Pahlavi Psalter fragments do not have special signature numbers, since they are unique in the Turfan Collection, but are referred to by folio number, e.g. Bl. 1.

66   See F. C. Andreas, "Bruchstücke einer Pehlewi-Übersetzung der Psalmen aus der Sassanidenzeit," *SPAW* (1910): 869-72; F. C. Andreas and Kaj Barr, "Bruchstücke einer Pehlewi-Übersetzung der Psalmen," *SPAW* (1933): 91-152; J. P. Asmussen, "Pahlavi Psalm 122 in English," in *Dr. J. M. Unvala Memorial Volume* (Bombay: Kaikhusroo M. JamaspAsa, 1964), 123-26; Philippe Gignoux, "Pahlavi Psalter," *Encyclopaedia Iranica Online*, available at http://www.iranicaonline.org/articles/pahlavi-psalter.

67   For a complete list of all fragments identified so far with their signature numbers, see Reck, "Survey of the Christian Sogdian Fragments," 192-193, 198.

68   In addition to Reck, "Survey of the Christian Sogdian Fragments," see Martin Schwartz, "Studies in the Texts of the Sogdian Christians" (Ph.D. diss., University of California, Berkeley, 1967), 126-44; Martin Schwartz, "Sogdian Fragments of the *Book of Psalms*," *AoF* 1 (1974): 257-61; Martin Schwartz, "Studies in the Texts of the Sogdian Christians (Revised Version)," (Ph.D. diss., University of California, Berkeley, 1982), 158-207.

69   **So 12955 (MIK III 56)** and **So 12950(2)**.

70   See Nicholas Sims-Williams, "A Greek-Sogdian Bilingual from Bulayïq," in *La Persia E Bisanzio* (Rome: Accademia Nazionale dei Lincei, 2004), 623-31; Reck, "Survey of the Christian Sogdian Fragments," 193. As noted above, these fragments suggest a possible origin in or at least connection with the Melkite Christian community in Tashkent, on which see Jean Dauvillier, "Byzantins d'Asie centrale et d'Extrême-orient au Moyen Age," *REB* 11 (1953): 62-87.

71   **MIK III 112** (T II B 57) and **SyrHT 153** (T II B 64).

72   See F. W. K. Müller, "Ein Syrisch-Neupersisches Psalmenbruchstück aus Chinesisch-Turkistan," in *Festschrift Eduard Sachau* (ed. Gotthold Weil; Berlin: Verlag von Georg Reimer, 1915), 215-22 and *Werner Sundermann, "Einige Bemerkungen zum Syrisch-Neupersischen Psalmenbruchstücke aus Chinesisch-Turkistan," in Mémorial Jean De Menasce* (ed. Philippe Gignoux and A. Tafazzoli; Louvain: Imprimerie Orientaliste, 1974), 441-52.

73   As Sims-Williams, "Christian Literature in Middle Iranian Languages," 277, n. 36 notes, "the other [side], which was perhaps originally the blank page at the beginning or end of the quire, was later used for the draft of a Syriac letter."

74   Maclean, *East Syrian Daily Offices*, 284-86; G. Diettrich, "Bericht über neuentdeckte handschriftliche Urkunden zur Geschichte des Gottesdienstes in

der nestorianischen Kirche," *NKGWG* (1909); F. Crawford Burkitt, "The Early Syriac Lectionary System," *PBA* 10 (1921-1923): 310, 328. As Burkitt notes, this reading is also found in BL Add. 14443, from the 6th/7th century.

[75] These books were translated into Syriac in the 6th century, after the Peshitta translation was finished, and are included in modern printed editions of the Syriac Bible.

[76] Matthew = 22 sections; Mark = 13 sections; Luke = 23 sections; John = 20 sections; Acts and General Epistles = 32 sections; Pauline Epistles = 55 sections.

[77] On lectionaries in the Syriac tradition, see Brock, *The Bible*, 50-51, 134-37.

[78] See also the following on fragments of a Syriac lectionary found at Dunhuang: Klein and Tubach, "Syrisch-Christliches Fragment" and Hubert Kaufhold, "Anmerkungen zur Veröffentlichung eines Syrischen Lektionarfragments," *ZDMG* 146 (1996): 49-60.

[79] Maclean, *East Syrian Daily Offices*, 288.

[80] Maclean, *East Syrian Daily Offices*, 289.

[81] Maclean, *East Syrian Daily Offices*, 289.

[82] See Gudrun Engberg, "Ekphonetic [Lectionary] Notation," *Grove Music Online*, available at www.oxfordmusiconline.com/subscriber/article/grove/music/08680, especially section 1. Syriac, Pehlevi and Soghdian. The recitation accents on the Syriac-Sogdian lectionary fragments are discussed in Egon Wellesz, "Miscellanea zur orientalistischen Musikgeschichte," *ZM* I (1919): 505-15.

[83] Indeed, the extant Syriac rubric on **n212** has helped in the reconstruction of the rubric on three of the four fragments. Interestingly, unlike both **n212** and the four fragments making up this folio from **Lectionary "B,"** published examples of the East Syriac lectionary readings for the First Sunday in Advent begin at verse 5, not verse 1: Maclean, *East Syrian Daily Offices*, 287; Diettrich, "Bericht," 164.

[84] Maclean, *East Syrian Daily Offices*, 287.

[85] Maclean, *East Syrian Daily Offices*, 287; Burkitt, "Early Syriac Lectionary," 331. Diettrich does not include a summary table of readings, but this passage cannot be found anywhere in his article.

[86] Maclean, *East Syrian Daily Offices*, 287; Diettrich, "Bericht," 164.

[87] Maclean, *East Syrian Daily Offices*, 287.

[88] The numbers used, E1-E6, follow the system in the draft version of Sims-Williams, *Catalogue*, which the author has kindly shared with me. Although they are not likely to change, interested readers should consult the final version of the catalogue for full details of these lectionary fragments. These fragments have been transcribed, translated and discussed in F. W. K. Müller, "Neutestamentliche Bruchstücke in Soghdischer Sprache," *SPAW* (1907): 260-70; Müller, "Soghdische Texte I"; Werner Sundermann, "Nachlese zu F. W. K. Müllers „Soghdischen Texten I", 1. Teil," *AoF* 1 (1974): 217-55; Werner Sundermann, "Nachlese zu F. W. K. Müllers „Soghdischen Texten I", 2. Teil," *AoF* 3 (1975): 55-90; Werner Sundermann, "Nachlese zu F. W. K. Müllers „Soghdischen Texten I", 3. Teil," *AoF* 8 (1981): 169-225. See also the commentaries in Louis H. Gray, "New Testament Fragments from Turkestan,"

ExpTim 25 (1913-1914): 59-61; Anton Baumstark, "Neue soghdisch-nestorianische Bruchstücke," *OrChr* 4 (N.S.) (1915): 123-28; F. Crawford Burkitt, *The Religion of the Manichees* (Cambridge: Cambridge University Press, 1925), 119-25; Curt Peters, "Der Texte der Soghdischen Evangelienbruchstücke und das Problem der Pešitta," *OrChr* 33 (1936): 153-62.

89 Information from the draft version of Sims-Williams, *Catalogue*.

90 Maclean, *East Syrian Daily Offices*, xxx; Diettrich, "Bericht," 162; Burkitt, "Early Syriac Lectionary," 305, 324.

91 See Burkitt, *Religion of the Manichees*, 120-24.

92 Following Baumstark, "Neue soghdisch-nestorianische Bruchstücke," 125, this is identified in the draft version of Sims-Williams, *Catalogue* as "presumably the end of the Gospel for the 5th Friday of Lent."

93 Following Baumstark, "Neue soghdisch-nestorianische Bruchstücke," 126 and Burkitt, *Religion of the Manichees*, 124, this is identified in the draft version of Sims-Williams, *Catalogue* as "probably for a saint's day."

94 In the lectionaries published by Burkitt and Diettrich (6th and 17th centuries, respectively), this is the reading for the Commemoration of the Departed (Burkitt, "Early Syriac Lectionary," 331; Diettrich, "Bericht," 165).

95 Listed under "Days for which no special lessons are appointed in the lectionary" in Maclean, *East Syrian Daily Offices*, 282. The same reading occurs as part of that for the Commemoration of the Syrian Doctors (Maclean, *East Syrian Daily Offices*, 287; Diettrich, "Bericht," 165) or Tuesday in the Week of Rest after Easter (Burkitt, "Early Syriac Lectionary," 331).

96 Following Baumstark, "Neue soghdisch-nestorianische Bruchstücke," 125, this is identified in the draft version of Sims-Williams, *Catalogue* as "presumably part of the Gospel for the 2nd Friday of Lent." The same reading also occurs as part of that for the Sixth Sunday of the Apostles (Maclean, *East Syrian Daily Offices*, 287; Diettrich, "Bericht," 168) or Rogations in general (Burkitt, "Early Syriac Lectionary," 333).

97 Luke 12:35-50 is given in BL Add. 14528 as the reading for Monday in Holy Week (Burkitt, "Early Syriac Lectionary," 333), but the Turfan text reflects a different occasion, since it ends at verse 44 and is immediately followed by the next "unidentified" reading beginning with John 5:19, on which see the following note.

98 Subsequently suggested by Nicholas Sims-Williams as "an alternative reading for… the Commemoration of the Dead," based on the inclusion of this verse in that reading as cited in Maclean, *East Syrian Daily Offices*, 287 and Burkitt, "Early Syriac Lectionary," 334. For more complete discussion of these "unidentified" lectionary readings, the reader is directed to Sims-Williams, *Catalogue*.

99 See discussion of this figure in Nicholas Sims-Williams, "Baršabbā," *Encyclopaedia Iranica* 3:823. On the importance of Merv to the Church of the East, see Hunter, "Church of the East in Central Asia."

100 See footnote above, under **Antiochian Christianity at Turfan**, regarding this amulet and its publication in Hunter, "Traversing time and location."

101 All references from the Psalms give the numbering according to the Peshitta, with MT equivalents in parentheses where relevant. Verse numbers are according to the MT and therefore differ from those found in Western translations of the Bible, since the former often count the heading as verse 1, whereas the latter do not.

102 All references from the Psalms give the numbering according to the Peshitta, with MT equivalents in parentheses where relevant. Verse numbers are according to the MT and therefore differ from those found in Western translations of the Bible, since the former often count the heading as verse 1, whereas the latter do not.

103 The uncertainty is due to the fact that one side of the fragments n177 and n178 is blank (apart from some later scribbles in Arabic script), suggesting the beginning of a new gospel codex, beginning with Matthew 1.

104 Not including fragments published in Müller, "Soghdische Texte I" which are now lost.

105 Again, not including fragments published in Müller, "Soghdische Texte I" which are now lost.

John Chrysostom and the Johannine Jews

1 It is difficult to find a study on anti-Judaism and the Fourth Gospel that does not uncritically assume the Fourth Gospel has always engendered anti-Jewish, and later anti-Semitic, hostilities among its readers; see, for example, James D. G. Dunn, "The Embarrassment of History: Reflections on the Problem of 'Anti-Judaism' in the Fourth Gospel," in *Anti-Judaism and the Fourth Gospel* (ed. Reimund Bieringer, Didier Pollefeyt, and Frederique Vandcasteel-Vanneuville; Louisville: WJKP, 2001), 41-60. Believing that the historical reading of the Fourth Gospel "provides a check on and counter to that later anti-Judaism," Dunn highlights the importance of separating the gospel's original meaning ("the historical text read historically") from its anti-Jewish *Wirkungsgeschichte* ("the anti-Judaism of later Christian tradition that was mounted upon John's anti-Jewish texts" [ibid., 59]), but he makes no attempt to identify that ostensible anti-Jewish *Wirkungsgeschichte*. A few pages prior, he observes, The extent to which this tradition [of Christian anti-Semitism] has been inspired by or built upon anti-Jewish material in the New Testament is here not the issue. The point is that, throughout the history of the church, the New Testament, or at least certain New Testament passages, has been read and heard as justifying, authorizing, even requiring anti-Jewish and subsequently anti-Semitic policies. Those who insist that the New Testament can be read only through the tradition or liturgy or properly heard only within the church need to remember that the virulent anti-Jewish polemics of John Chrysostom and Martin Luther are also part of the tradition... (ibid., 55-6). There is little doubt that "anti-Jewish material in the New Testament" sometimes has led to anti-Jewish hostilities, but to assume such material was interpreted, without variation, in an anti-Judaic

manner by patristic writers such as Chrysostom is to underestimate the multivalent nature and goals of patristic exegesis.

2 For the English translation to which I refer below, see John Chrysostom, *Commentary on Saint John the Apostle and Evangelist* (trans. Thomas Aquinas Goggin; Fathers of the Church 33, 41; Washington, D.C.: The Catholic University of America Press, 1957, 1959). Unless otherwise cited, all translations in this paper are my own, based on the Greek text found in John Chrysostom, *Homilies on John*, Patrologia Graeca 59 (ed. Bernard de Montfaucon; Paris, 1862).

3 For one such project, see Fred Allen Grissom, "Chrysostom and the Jews: Studies in Jewish-Christian Relations in Fourth-Century Antioch" (Ph.D. diss., The Southern Baptist Theological Seminary, 1978). Most other studies related to John Chrysostom and the Jews focus almost exclusively on his *Adversus Judaeos*. The best such example remains Robert Louis Wilken, *John Chrysostom and the Jews: Rhetoric and Reality in the Late Fourth Century* (Berkeley: University of California Press, 1983).

4 Karen Jo Torjesen's analysis of Origen's hermeneutical method has been tremendously influential in my own realization of this point with regards to Chrysostom (*Hermeneutical Procedure and Theological Structure in Origen's Exegesis*, Patristische Texte und Studien 28 [Berlin: De Gruyter, 1986]).

5 Cf. *Hom. Jo.* 4 (FC 33, 44); 13 (FC 33, 119-121); 22 (FC 33, 212); 25 (FC 33, 242); 30 (FC 33, 295-6); 32 (FC 33, 321); 52 (FC 41, 54).

6 Cf. *Hom. Jo.* 14 (FC 33, 139-140); 12 (FC 33, 110); 76 (FC 41, 321-2).

7 Cf. *Hom. Jo.* 50 (FC 41, 29).

8 Cf. Francis M. Young's enlightening discussion of Chrysostom's homilies on 1 Corinthians (*Biblical Exegesis and the Formation of Christian Culture* [Peabody, Mass.: Hendrickson, 2002], 248-257), to which I remain indebted for many of my own observations with regards to his homilies on John.

9 *Hom. Jo.* 38 (PG 59:218). Cf. *Hom. Jo.* 28 (FC 33, 275-7).

10 Cf. John 5:41-44; 7:18; 8:50-54.

11 Cf. *Hom. Jo.* 57 and 69 (FC 41, 243).

12 Cf. *Hom. Jo.* 3, 8, and 35.

13 Cf.. *Hom. Jo.* 20, 23, 35, 37, and 38. Cf. *Hom. Jo.* 16 regarding the Jews' envy of John the Baptist.

14 *Hom. Jo.* 55 (PG 59:306).

15 Cf. *Hom. Jo.* 31.

16 *Hom. Jo.* 48 (PG 59:269).

17 Chrysostom frequently distinguishes between the crowds and the leaders in order to highlight the end to which a simple-minded, though not sinful, crowd would be led by the vices of their leaders. Commenting on the positive interest of the Jews in Jesus in John 12, Chrysostom observes, "Just as wealth is wont to ruin those who are not paying attention, so it is with also with power; for the former leads to greediness and the latter to desperation. Notice, for instance, how the multitude of the Jews, who were subject to authority, were sound, while

their rulers were corrupt" (*Hom. Jo.* 66 [PG 59:365]). Cf. *Hom. Jo.* 57 (FC 41, 102-3).

[18] The danger of envy and jealousy, for Chrysostom, is their likeliness to lead even to murder: "the tyranny of jealously has overturned entire churches and destroyed the whole world; it is the mother of murder" (*Hom. Jo.* 38 [PG 59:211]). Cf. *Hom. Jo.* 49 (FC 41, 12-3).

[19] *Hom. Jo.* 47 (PG 59:268). Elsewhere, Chrysostom equates one's partaking of the mysteries of Christ unworthily with being guilty of the body and blood of Christ (*Hom. Jo.* 60 [PG 59:334]).

[20] *Hom. Jo.* 48 (PG 59:273). Cf. *Hom. Jo.* 37 (FC 33, 365).

[21] Cf. *Hom. Jo.* 54 especially, but also *Hom. Jo.* 18 (FC 33, 190); 21 (FC 33, 209-11); 25 (FC 33, 248); 48 (FC 41, 6).

[22] Cf. *Hom. Jo.* 11 (FC 33, 103-6); 16 (FC 33, 159-160); 45 (FC 33, 452); 43 (FC 33, 440); 81 (FC 41, 384).

[23] Cf. *Hom. Jo.* 6-8, 25, and 54.

[24] *Hom. Jo.* 47 (FC 33, 480 [PG 59:266]). Cf. *Hom. Jo.* 47 (FC 33, 477-8).

[25] Examples abound. Cf. *Hom. Jo.* 11, 16, and 43.

[26] *Hom. Jo.* 6 (FC 33, 72 [PG 59:61]).

[27] *Hom. Jo.* 7 (FC 33, 74 [PG 59:61]).

[28] Cf. *Hom. Jo.* 39 (FC 33, 397-8).

[29] Cf. Young, *Biblical Exegesis,* 165-9.

[30] Chrysostom frequently suggests that the gospel's contents may be intended more for later generations than for Christ's or the evangelist's contemporaries. Cf. *Hom. Jo.* 34 (FC 33, 332); 42; 49 (FC 41, 13); 59 (FC 41, 123); 61 (FC 41, 154); 78 (FC 41, 340); 83 (FC 41, 408); 88 (FC 41, 474).

[31] Cf. *Hom. Jo.* 39-41 and 76.

[32] *Hom. Jo.* 24 (PG 59:144). Cf. *Hom. Jo.* 26 (PG 59:155).

[33] *Hom. Jo.* 30 (PG 59:173).

[34] *Hom. Jo.* 70 (PG 59:384).

[35] As has been noted frequently, Chrysostom's homilies on John are more doctrinal and theological than usual. In Chrysostom's understanding, Jesus in John even speaks *directly* to later heretics (e.g. *Hom. Jo.* 22 [PG 59:135; FC 33, 216]). As such, Chrysostom directs his exegesis against Marcion and his followers (cf. *Hom. Jo.* 85 [FC 41, 433]), Paul of Samosata and his followers (cf. *Hom. Jo.* 8 [FC 33, 82-3]; 39 [FC 33, 393]; 48 [FC 33, 4]), Manicheans (cf. *Hom. Jo.* 22 [FC 33, 216] and 46 [FC 33, 463]), Sabellius and Arius (cf. *Hom. Jo.* 82 [FC 41, 392]; 38; 39 [FC 33, 389]), Greeks and pagans (cf. *Hom. Jo.* 17 [FC 33, 170]; 27 [FC 33, 265]; 28 [FC 33, 275-6]; 60 [FC 41, 224]; 63 [FC 41, 186]; 72), those who disbelieve the resurrection (*Hom. Jo.* 39 [FC 33, 395]), and heretics in general (*Hom. Jo.* 15, 39, 47 and 85). For Chrysostom, Nicodemus is representative primarily of heretics who subject the things of God to their own reason (*Hom. Jo.* 24). To further oppose contemporary heretics, Chrysostom frequently and anachronistically paints Jesus as a good, orthodox theologian (e.g. *Hom. Jo.* 39). If Jesus' words lead one to suspect otherwise, it is only because Jesus "condescended" to his audience and used words more affable to

the human—especially Jewish—ear in order to communicate his divinity tactfully (cf. *Hom. Jo.* 30 [FC 33, 290] and 38 [FC 33, 380]). Such "condescension" or "considerateness" (συγκατάβασις; e.g. *Hom. Jo.* 39 [PG 59:221]) is fundamental to Chrysostom's understanding of Scripture.

[36] "He spoke these things, urging them to faith, as he had done earlier, when he said, 'Still a little while I am with you. The one who walks in darkness does not know where he is going' [cf. Jn 12:35]. What things the Jews in our day are doing yet do not see what they are doing! Walking as if in darkness, they think they are traveling on the straight road, but they are walking on the opposite: keeping the Sabbath, guarding the law, and observing food regulations. They do not see where they walk. This is why he said, 'Walk in the light, that you might become sons of light' [Jn 12.35], that is to say, 'my sons'" (*Hom. Jo.* 68 [PG 59:374]).

[37] Cf. *Hom. Jo.* 83-88.

[38] *Hom. Jo.* 88 (PG 59:481).

[39] Such a position—that the Fourth Gospel expresses deep-seated hostility—frequently is predicated on a supposed historical split, of varying degrees, between "church" and "synagogue," in which the Johannine community had been excluded from its parent synagogue. This sort of historical division was especially popularized by J. Louis Martyn (*History and Theology in the Fourth Gospel*, 3rd ed. The New Testament Library [Louisville: WJKP, 2003], first published in 1968), but the extent of this division has come under increasing scrutiny in recent scholarship. Nonetheless, even scholars who question the extent of the separation continue to assert that the feelings expressed in the Fourth Gospel are at the very least *hostile*, likely in response to some sort of exclusion. Two examples include Tina Pippin, "'For Fear of the Jews': Lying and Truth-Telling in Translating the Gospel of John," *Semeia* 76 (1996): 81-97 and Adele Reinhartz, "'Jews' and Jews in the Fourth Gospel," in *Anti-Judaism and the Fourth Gospel* (ed. Reimund Bieringer, et al.), 213-227. For slightly contrary perspectives, see Luke Timothy Johnson, "The New Testament's Anti-Jewish Slander and the Conventions of Ancient Polemic," *Journal of Biblical Literature* 108 (1989): 419-41 as well as Stephen Motyer, *Your Father the Devil? A New Approach to John and 'the Jews'* (Carlisle, UK: Carlisle Paternoster, 1997). For an especially illuminating discussion of the identity of "the Jews" in the Fourth Gospel, see Daniel Boyarin, "The Ioudaioi in John and the Prehistory of 'Judaism'," in *Pauline Conversations in Context: Essays in Honor of Calvin J. Roetzel* (ed. Janice Capel Anderson, Philip Sellew, and Claudia Setzer; Sheffield: Sheffield Academic Press, 2002), 216-39.

[40] Cf. *Hom. Jo.* 61 (PG 59:337).

[41] *Hom. Jo.* 49 (PG 59:278).

Theōria as a Hermeneutical Term

1   "The watchword of the Antiochian school was *theōria*, from a Greek word meaning 'to see.' They contended that the spiritual sense was in no way separable from the literal sense, as it was in the Alexandrian school. The exegetes of the Antiochian school were united in their single-minded concern to preserve the integrity of history and the natural sense of a passage. But they were just as concerned about being overly literalistic as about the excesses of allegory and what they called 'Judaism.' Both extremes were equally dangerous; only *theōria* could offer the middle road out of the dangers on both sides" (Walter C. Kaiser and Moisés Silva, *Introduction to Biblical Hermeneutics: The Search for Meaning* [rev. ed.; Grand Rapids: Zondervan, 2007], 266). Antiochene *theōria* is not to be confused with the mystical *theoria* of the Alexandrian school (cf. Edmund J. Rybarczyk, *Beyond Salvation: Eastern Orthodoxy and Classical Pentecostalism on Becoming Like Christ* [Eugene, Ore.: Wipf and Stock, 2004], 29n25). But the use even among the Antiochenes is not monolithic. For example Nassif notes that "Chrysostom knew *theōria* as the divine revelation or mystical illumination of spiritual realities which attended the processes of inscripturation, interpretation, or homiletical discourse. The Antiochene pastor utilized the hermeneutic to describe the nature of the prophetic experience as an inspired revelation of heavenly realities or of deeper Christian truths. Quite unlike Theodore of Mopsuestia or Diodore of Tarsus's hyperbolic method of messianic prophecy, Chrysostom generally uproots such prophecies as Zechariah 9:9 from their historical setting and interprets them as direct prophecies of Christ. However like Diodore, his exegetical tutor, Chrysostom also applied *theōria* to the interpretive task of disclosing the soteriological significance of typological relationships and a broad range of narrative statements and figures of speech in Scripture" (Bradley Nassif, "The 'Spiritual Exegesis' of Scripture: The School of Antioch Revisited," *ATR* 75, no. 4 [Fall 1993]: 457).

2   Primary sources for this research include manuscripts of Theodore's and Theodoret's exegetical works found in the Thesaurus Linguae Graecae (TLG) database, a digital library of Greek literature from the time of Homer (850 B.C.E.) to about 1450 C.E. located at the University of California, Irvine and online at www.tlg.uci.edu. J.-P. Minge, *Patrologiae Cursus Completus (Series Graeca)* (Paris: Migne, 1857–1866) (PG) was also regularly consulted. These sources are supplemented with recent translations especially from The Fathers of the Church (FC) multivolume series and from the catenae of The Ancient Christian Commentary on Scripture (ACCS). The first is published by Catholic University of America, the second by InterVarsity.

3   Bradley Nassif, "Antiochene 'Theoria' in John Chrysostom's Exegesis" (Ph.D. diss., Fordham University, 1991).

4   Cf. Nassif, "The 'Spiritual Exegesis' of Scripture," 469–470.

5   Bertrand de Margerie, *An Introduction to the History of Exegesis [The Greek Fathers, Volume I]* (1st ed.; Petersham, Mass.: St. Bede's, 2002), 170. For purposes of this study, it will be granted that both Theodore's and Theodoret's

writings fall into the classification of Antiochene exegesis, albeit on opposite sides of that spectrum. For interaction for and against this position see Richard J. Perhai, "Antiochene *Theoria* in the Writings of Theodore of Mopsuestia and Theodoret of Cyrus: A Paradigm for Theological Interpretation" (Ph.D. diss., Baptist Bible Seminary, 2012), 25–42.

[6] E.g., Frederic William Farrar, *History of Interpretation* (London: Macmillan, 1886), 210–211, 213–219; and Milton Terry, *Biblical Hermeneutics: A Treatise on the Interpretation of the Old and New Testaments*, 2d ed. (New York; Grand Rapids: Hunt and Eaton; Zondervan, 1890, reprint 1978), 647–651.

[7] E.g, Margaret M. Mitchell, "Patristic Rhetoric on Allegory: Origen and Eustathius Put 1 Samuel 28 on Trial," *The Journal of Religion* 85, no. 3 (July 2005): 414–445.

[8] That is, *theōria* helps them to see "the spiritual sense . . . in no way separable from the literal sense" (Kaiser and Silva, *Introduction to Biblical Hermeneutics*, rev. ed., 266).

[9] I maintain this despite disagreement by some scholars. For interaction with key patristic scholars (some who reject or nuance the distinction between Antiochene *theōria* and Alexandrian ἀλληγορία) see Perhai, "Antiochene *Theoria* in the Writings of Theodore and Theodoret," chap. 3.

[10] Cf. Adam M. Schor, "Theodoret on the 'School of Antioch': A Network Approach," *Journal of Early Christian Studies* 15, no. 4 (Winter 2007): 517–40, 542–43, 545–60, 562; idem, *Theodoret's People: Social Networks and Religious Conflict in Late Roman Syria* (Berkeley, Calif.: University of California Press, 2011); and Perhai, "Antiochene *Theoria* in the Writings of Theodore and Theodoret," 25–54.

[11] For an outline of their family backgrounds, education, and especially the specific historical exigencies that influence their exegetical writings, see Frances M. Young and Andrew Teal, *From Nicaea to Chalcedon: A Guide to the Literature and Its Background,* 2d ed. (Grand Rapids: Baker, 2010), 261–264, 322–327; cf. Perhai, "Antiochene *Theoria* in the Writings of Theodore and Theodoret," 42–54.

[12] Robert C. Hill, trans., *Diodore of Tarsus: Commentary on Psalms 1–51* (Leiden; Boston: Brill, 2005), xi.

[13] Ibid., xi–xii. Hill, however, is convinced that Diodore both misunderstood Alexandrian ἀλληγορία and was imprecise in his distinctions between ἱστορικόν and ἀλληγορικόν (ibid., xii, xxv). Hill seeks refuge under Frances Young's contention that ἱστορικόν "was not 'historical' in the modern sense." (ibid., xxv n. 42, citing Frances M. Young, *Biblical Exegesis and the Formation of Christian Culture* [Cambridge: Cambridge University Press, 1997], 168). In so doing, Hill seems to miss the point; namely, *for Diodore the narrative* (ἱστορικόν) *stood on its own as coherent revelation that really occurred without need for symbolic embellished* (ἀλληγορικόν). For moral benefit (i.e., to move from historical meaning to application for his readers) Diodore uses the term θεωρία ten times in the preface to his *Commentary on Psalms* (TLG 4134.004 lines 127, 128, 131–133, 135 [2x], 137, 154, 156; for an English translation see

Hill, *Diodore's Commentary on Psalms 1–51*, 4–5). Various translations of Diodore's distinction between *theōria* and ἀλληγορία found in this preface are regularly cited by scholars as the key (albeit usually the only) explanation of Antiochene *theōria* (cf. J. N. D. Kelly, *Early Christian Doctrines* [5th ed.; San Francisco: Harper & Row, 1976], 76–77; Dimitri Z. Zaharopoulos, *Theodore of Mopsuestia on the Bible: A Study of His Old Testament Exegesis* [New York; Mahwah, N.J.: Paulist Press, 1989], 111; Christoph Schäublin, *Untersuchungen zu Methode und Herkunft der antiochenischen Exegese* [Theophania 23; Köln-Bonn: Peter Hanstein, 1974], 84, 156; Rowan A. Greer, *Theodore of Mopsuestia, Exegete and Theologian* [Westminster, U.K.: Faith Press, 1961], 93; G. W. Ashby, "Theodoret of Cyrrhus as Exegete of the Old Testament" [Ph.D. diss., Rhodes University, 1972], 22; Frances Young, "Alexandrian and Antiochene Exegesis," in *A History of Biblical Interpretation: The Ancient Period* [ed. Alan J. Hauser and Duane F. Watson; Grand Rapids: Eerdmans, 2003], 1:347; Frederick G. McLeod, *Theodore of Mopsuestia* [London; New York: Routledge, 2009], 21; Karlfried Froehlich, ed., *Biblical Interpretation in the Early Church* [Philadelphia: Fortress, 1984], 85; Anthony C. Thiselton, *Hermeneutics: An Introduction* [Grand Rapids: Eerdmans, 2009], 110; Jean-Noël Guinot, "La frontière entre allégorie et typologie: École Alexandrine, École Antiochienne," *Recherches de science religieuse* 99, no. 2 [2011]: 213). Perhaps this was encouraged by Minge's Latin work on Theodore. There Minge begins his *De Duobus Theodori Libris Argumenti Hermeneutici*, with a discussion of the hermeneutical distinction between allegory and *theōria* in Theodore and Diodore's writings (PG 66.25–26).

14 Zaharopoulos, *Theodore of Mopsuestia on the Bible*, 42n69. Theodore also writes a *Commentary on the Nicene Creed* and *Commentary on the Lord's Prayer* which provides a goldmine of his theological perspectives (Theodore of Mopsuestia, Commentary of Theodore of Mopsuestia on the Nicene Creed, ed. and trans. Alphonse Mingana [Woodbrooke Studies; Cambridge: Heffer, 1932]; idem, Commentary of Theodore of Mopsuestia on the Lord's Prayer, Baptism and the Eucharist, ed. and trans. Alphonse Mingana [Woodbrooke Studies; Cambridge: Heffer, 1933]) in the public domain along with other rare early church father works (Roger Pearse, ed., "Early Church Fathers–Additional Texts," http://www.tertullian.org/fathers/ [accessed November 11, 2008]). Some other fragments of Theodore's doctrinal writings remain, e.g., *On the Incarnation*, in PG 66.972–992, translated in McLeod, *Theodore of Mopsuestia*, 126–147.

15 Facundus of Hermianae, *Pro defensione trium capitulorum* 3.6 (PL 67.602); PG 66.648–696; cf. *Theodore of Mopsuestia: Commentary on Psalms 1–81*, trans. Robert C. Hill (Atlanta, Ga.:SBL, 2006); Theodore of Mopsuestia, *Commentary on the Twelve Prophets,* trans. Robert C. Hill (FC 108; Washington, D.C.: Catholic University of America, 2004), 3n12.

16 PG 66.124–632; H. N. Sprenger, *Theodori Mopsuesteni Commentarius in XII Prophetetas*. Biblica et Patristica 1 (Göttinger Orientforschungen, Wiesbaden:

Otto Harrassowtiz, 1977); Theodore of Mopsuestia, *Commentary on the Twelve Prophets*.

[17] PG 66.728–786; George Kalantzis, *Theodore of Mopsuestia: Commentary on the Gospel of John* (Strathfield, Aus.: St. Pauls, 2004) is based on the Greek.

[18] Mathew in PG 66.705–713. Mark in PG 66.713–716. Luke in PG 66.716–728. Romans in PG 66.787–876. 1 Corinthians in PG 877–894. 2 Corinthians in PG 66.894–898. Galatians in PG 66.898–912. Ephesians in PG 66.912–921. Philippians in PG 66.921–925. Colossians in PG 66.925–932. 1–2 Thessalonians in PG 66.932–936. 1 Timothy in PG 66.936–944. 2 Timothy in PG 66.945–948. Titus in PG 66.948–949. Philemon in PG 66.949. Hebrews in PG 66.952–968. For Greek fragments on Genesis and Exodus see PG 66.636–648.

[19] For details see TLG under Canon Author # 4135 (or Author Theodorus Mopsuestenus), which offers twelve primary sources in Greek. For a full listing of Theodore's writings, many not extant, see Ebedjesus, *Catalogue des livres ecclésiastiques syriens*, in *Bibliotheca Orientalis* III, ed. J. S. Assemani (Rome: Typis S. C. de Propaganda Fida, 1926), 30–35. For those extant see Zaharopoulos, *Theodore of Mopsuestia on the Bible*, 1–2; 27–35. For more details on the chronology of Theodore's writings see J.-M. Voste, "La chronologie de l'activite de Theodore de Mopsueste au II Councile de Constantinople," *RB* 34 (January 1925): 54–81.

[20] Brevard S. Childs, *The Struggle to Understand Isaiah as Christian Scripture* (Grand Rapids: Eerdmans, 2004), 134.

[21] Theodoret, *Epistle 16* (NPNF2, 3.2).

[22] NPNF2, 3.3; Young and Teal, *From Nicaea to Chalcedon*, 323–324. Apparently Syrian Apamea on the Orontes River about 65 miles south of Syrian Antioch.

[23] NPNF2, 3.4; Johannes Quasten, *Patrology, Vol. 3: The Golden Age of Greek Patristic Literature* (4th ed.; Westminster, Md.: Christian Classics, 1984), 536.

[24] The ultra-Arians argued for the complete "intelligibility of the Divine Essence," i.e., God without mystery, and so denied the deity of the Holy Spirit (along with the Son). But they adhered to the full humanity of Christ unlike the Apollinarians (NPNF2, 14.175).

[25] The ultra-Arians argued for the complete "intelligibility of the Divine Essence," i.e., God without mystery, and so denied the deity of the Holy Spirit (along with the Son). But they adhered to the full humanity of Christ unlike the Apollinarians (NPNF2, 14.175).

[26] NPNF2, 3.8–11; Trevor A. Hart, ed., The Dictionary of Historical Theology (Carlisle, Cumbria, U.K.: Paternoster, 2000), 540; Young and Teal, From Nicaea to Chalcedon, 324–326.

[27] NPNF2, 14.300, 302–324; Tony Lane, *A Concise History of Christian Thought* (rev. and exp. ed.; Grand Rapids: Baker, 2006), 54; de Margerie, *An Introduction to the History of Exegesis I*, 182.

[28] TLG includes 25 Greek sources. Cf. NPNF2, 3.14–24 for a fuller list of his writings.

29 For details see TLG under Canon Author # 4089 and Quasten, *Patrology,*
     3.538–554.

30 Robert C. Hill, trans., *Theodoret of Cyrus: Commentary on the Psalms, 1–72*
     (FC; Washington, D.C.: Catholic University of America, 2000), 40.

31 Theodoret, *The Song of Songs, Translated into English Verse: With an
     Introduction from St. Athanasius, Notes From Theodoret, and Appendix from St.
     Bernard* (London: Rivingtons, 1864).

32 PG 81.1255–1545; Robert C. Hill, ed., *Theodoret of Cyrus: Commentary on
     Daniel,* trans. Robert C. Hill (Atlanta, Ga.: SBL, 2006).

33 PG 81. 807–1254; Robert C Hill, *Theodoret of Cyrus: Commentary on the
     Prophets: Commentary on the Prophet Ezekiel (Commentaries on the Prophets)*
     (Holy Cross Orthodox Press, 2007).

34 Robert C. Hill, trans., *Theodoret of Cyrus: Commentaries on the Prophets:
     Commentaries on Jeremiah, Baruch and the Book of Lamentations* (vol. 1, 3
     vols.; Brookline, Mass.: Holy Cross Orthodox Press, 2007).

35 PG 80.857–1998; Hill, *Commentary on the Psalms, 1–72*; Robert C. Hill, trans.,
     Theodoret of Cyrus: Commentary on the Psalms, 73–150 (FC 102; Washington,
     D.C.: Catholic University of America, 2001).

36 Theodoret of Cyrus, *The Questions on the Octateuch: On Genesis and Exodus,*
     ed. John F. Petruccione; trans. Robert C. Hill (Washington, D.C.: Catholic
     University of America, 2007); Theodoret of Cyrus, *Theodoret of Cyrus, the
     Questions on the Octateuch: On Leviticus, Numbers, Deuteronomy, Joshua,
     Judges, and Ruth,* trans. Robert C. Hill (Washington, D.C.: Catholic University
     of America, 2007). For a summary of the dating of all Theodoret's earlier works
     cf. Jean-Noël Guinot, *L'Exegésè de Théodoret de Cyr* (Théologie Historique
     100; Paris: Beauchesne, 1995), 62–63.

37 Note that TLG takes Theodore, *Commentary on the Twelve Prophets* from
     Sprenger, *Theodori Mopsuesteni commentarius in XII Prophetas,* 1–429. Hill
     uses both this source as well as PG 66.124–632 (Theodore of Mopsuestia,
     Commentary on the Twelve Prophets, 5). Throughout Hill's translation, he
     references only the pages from PG rather than Sprenger. This at times makes it
     difficult to cross-reference the TLG version with PG.

38 The analysis in this chapter should enhance the reader's understanding of
     Antiochene interpretation. For a complete development of this analysis for both
     Theodore and Theodoret see Perhai, "Antiochene *Theoria* in the Writings of
     Theodore and Theodoret," 54–80.

39 For an analysis of Diodore's use of *theōria* (German: *Schau*) in his exegesis and
     the preface to his *Com. on Psalms* cf. Felix Thome, *Historia contra Mythos: die
     Schriftauslegung Diodors von Tarsus und Theodors von Mopsuestia im
     Widerstreit zu Kaiser Julians und Salustius' allegorischem Mythenverständnis*
     (Bonn: Borengässer, 2004), 89, 97–101, 113–119. Unfortunately, Thome pro-
     vides little explicit treatment of *Schau* in Theodore's writings in this work.

40 Theodore's uses of the verbal form *theōreo* are confined to the semantic range
     "seeing" and "observing." Cf. Hill, *Theodore of Mopsuestia: Commentary on
     Psalms 1–81,* xxxii–xxxiii, 911n4, where the term is only used by Hill (the

editor) in his preface and in a footnote of Hill's translation of Ps 69:21, as an interpretive method Theodore did *not* use.

41 Since Psalm 110 in Theodore's commentary is not extant, we must rely on secondary sources for this information. Zaharopoulos does not provide a source (Zaharopoulos, *Theodore of Mopsuestia on the Bible*, 168). Robert Hill point to Diodore as the source (Robert C. Hill, "His Master's Voice: Theodore of Mopsuestia on the Psalms," *The Heythrop Journal* 45, no. 1 [January 2004]: 45).

42 Theodore of Mopsuestia, *Commentary on the Twelve Prophets*, 118–119.

43 This is because these events did not happen indeed to David or any other Jew of his day.

44 Theodore uses the term ὑπερβολικῶς 11 times in his writings: Ps 57:4a, line 7; Joel 2:28–32 lines 34, 44, 72; Zeph 1:3 line 1; Zech 9:9–10b lines 1, 9; and 14:1–2 line 20 (TLG). Of these Zech 9:9–10 is most significant and similar to his treatment of Psalm 69:10. There he also treats the third promise of the Abrahamic covenant (Gen 26:4), and God's promise in the Davidic covenant (Ps 89:36–37) akin. I.e., they are only hyperbolically or metaphorically realized in their near referents (the nations of Israel and David's line, respectively), but "the factual reality of the text"—the true or ultimate referent—is Christ Jesus. See Theodore of Mopsuestia, *Commentary on the Twelve Prophets*, 108:367; cf. 172; Alberto Vaccari, "La Θεωρια Nella Scuola Esegetica Di Antiochia," *Biblica* 1 (January 1920): 18–19; and Nassif, "The 'Spiritual Exegesis' of Scripture," 443–444, 77, 52–54. However, Theodore uses other forms of ὑπερβολ* 44 more times. And, not surprisingly, Theodore uses the term μεταφορικῶς less—only 6 times located in his commentaries at Ps 41:8b line 3; 73;13c line 3; Joel 2;28–32 lines 44, 53, 71; and Gospel of John fragment 35 line 14 (TLG). A search for ὑπερβολ* near θεωρ* within 10 lines for Theodore found instances only in Theodore's commentary following Hos 2:2. But it proves to be a mundane use of *theōreo* (cf. Theodore of Mopsuestia, *Commentary on the Twelve Prophets*, 45–46). In contrast, Theodoret uses the term ὑπερβολικῶς only 7 times in all of his TLG writings: Ps 118:10 (PG 81.812.37) theoretical–Israel and Church; Heb 5:7–10 (PG 82.713 lines 3 and 7) in relation to the Incarnate one suffering; Ezek 31:3 (PG 81.1117.50); Hab 2:11 (PG 81.1821.26) 1 Cor 13:1 (PG 82.332.46); 1 Cor 13:3 (PG 82.333.31) all hyperbole without any theoretic prophetic interpretation. Only in Ps 118:10 does Theodoret explicitly describe his interpretation as partially applying to a near referent (in this case Israel) but fully to a later referent (in this case the Church). So relative to the number of words in each corpus, Theodore uses the term 1.7 times more often. But Theodoret uses other forms of ὑπερβολ* 230 more times, too many to analyze here. For Theodoret with the same search (ὑπερβολ* near θεωρ* within 10 lines before or after) reveals 3 instances at: Ezek 5:7–10 (PG 81.865.5); Ps 30 (PG 80.1081.25), but *theōreo* is from the biblical verse there; and Ps 58 (PG 80.1309.6) but προθεωρία (preface) in one verse and ὑπερβολή in the next (*Pauline Epist.* [*PG*, n.d., 82.608.47). I.e., these are all mundane uses the *theōria* or *theōreo*.

45 Theodore of Mopsuestia, *Commentary on the Twelve Prophets*, 108:226–227; cf. Nassif, "Antiochene '*Theoria*' in John Chrysostom's Exegesis," 54; and Vaccari, "La Θεωρια Nella Scuola Esegetica di Antiochia," 19–20. Theodore shows himself as a contemplative historian in this passage comparing the lives of David's descendants to Jesus.

46 Theodore of Mopsuestia, *Commentary on the Twelve Prophets*, 118. Theodore also gets this idea of shadow versus substance from Col 2:17; Heb 8:5, and 10:1 since the Antiochenes sought to follow the interpretive (and theological) examples of the NT authors, especially Paul.

47 Theodore uses the term *theōria* in verse one of Obadiah as he discusses the phrase *Vision of Obadiah*. "This differs not at all in its import from the phrase 'word of the Lord': Scripture calls God's activity 'word of the Lord' in reference to the spiritual grace by which the prophets received the revelations of the future, and in the same way by *vision* he refers to the divine revelation by which in fact they received the knowledge of the unknown. Since, you see, they received also some insights [*theōria*] in ineffable fashion through spiritual activity in their own soul, and in response to the activity occurring within them from the Holy Spirit they obeyed the instruction in what was said as though from someone speaking, consequently Scripture calls it both vision and 'word of the Lord,' and probably also 'report,' in that they receive knowledge as though by a report of some kind" Ibid., 176–177. Robert Hill in his translations italicizes (rather than placing in quotation marks) words that are part of the biblical text. (They will be italicized herein without further comment.) Here Theodore explains the prophets' receiving revelation either by way of a direct "word of the Lord" or by way of vision. Apparently both of these means of revelation could be accompanied by an unexplainable (ἀπορρήτως) work of the Spirit in the prophet (any OT writer). This process Theodore calls *theōria*.

48 Thus more than half of the instances of *theōria* in Theodore's extant Greek writings on TLG are located in TLG 4135.007 (cf. PG 66.401.47, 51, 53; 66.404.1, 4, 6, 47, 52).

49 οὕτω δυνηθῆναι τῇ τῶν δεικνυμένων θεωρίᾳ προσανέχειν μόνῃ (from PG 66.401.46–47). Hill translates it in the larger context, "It was by ecstasy, therefore, that in all likelihood they all received the knowledge of things beyond description, since it was possible for them in their minds to be quite removed from their normal condition and thus capable of devoting themselves exclusively to contemplation [*theōria*] of what was revealed" (Theodore of Mopsuestia, *Commentary on the Twelve Prophets*, 249).

50 Such contemplation is required by the nature of the revelation itself as well as for the writing down of the concursively inspired revelation. For more on concursive inspiration see Benjamin B. Warfield, *The Works of Benjamin B. Warfield, Volume 1: Revelation and Inspiration* (Bellingham, Wash.: Logos Bible Software, 2008), 15–16, 26–28. Cf. Bertrand de Margerie, use of the phrase "contemplative historians" (de Margerie, *An Introduction to the History of Exegesis I*, 165–170, esp. 167). He uses this description to refer to the prophets who consider their own time and future messianic fulfillment. This

writer affirms de Margerie's description as expressing the first aspect of *theōria*, while suggesting that "contemplative historians" applies as well to the second aspect of *theoria* of (NT) authors meditating on Scripture and the Spirit speaking to them through that to reveal new words from God. Nassif finds a similar view for Chrysostom who viewed inspiration as a divine-human process (Nassif, "Antiochene 'Theoria' in John Chrysostom's Exegesis," 174–177).

51 Theodore of Mopsuestia, *Commentary on the Twelve Prophets*, 249; cf. Nassif, "Antiochene 'Theoria' in John Chrysostom's Exegesis," 82.

52 Those who have spent time laboring over research for a dissertation, however, may well understand the sense of being disconnected from the perception of mundane realities around them in order to focus their attention solely on their research.

53 Theodore of Mopsuestia, *Commentary on the Twelve Prophets*, 249–250 (PG 66.401.54–66.404.6).

54 Patristic and biblical scholars point to the preface of Theodore's *Com. on Jonah* as illustrative of his Christian or "theoretic" interpretation. E.g., Charlotte Köckert—in a manner quite similar to my observation of the threefold (OT prophet, NT author, post-canonical interpreter) aspect of Antiochene *theōria*— writes, „Theodore bietet somit im Proömium Kommentars einerseits eine lehrhaft-moralische, andererseits eine christologisch-typologische Deutung der Jona-Geschehen als historisches Ereignis auf und leitet aus ihm einen dreifachen Nutzen ab: Im historischen Kontext Jonas bewirkt es Umkehr und Rettung für die Bewohner Ninives; für die Zeit des Alten Bundes bietet es Unterweisung und Seelsorge für die Propheten; in der Zeit nach der Ankunft Christi dient es zur Mahnung, Unterweisung und Glaubensstärkung für christliche Leser." ("Theodore therefore offers in the preface of the commentary on the one hand didactic and moral, on the other hand, a Christological and typological interpretation of the Jonah events as a historic event leads to and from it from a triple benefit: In the historical context Jonas brings to repentance and salvation for the inhabitants of Nineveh, for the time of the Old Testament, it provides instruction and pastoral care for the prophets, in the period after the coming of Christ, it serves as a reminder, training and strengthening of faith for Christian readers") (Charlotte Köckert. "Der Jona-Kommentar des Theodor von Mopsuestia. Eine christliche Jona-Auslegung an der Wende zum 5. Jahrhundert (mit einer Übersetzung des Kommentars)," in *Der problematische Prophet: die biblische Jona-Figur in Exegese, Theologie, Literatur und bildender Kunst*, ed. Johann Anselm Steiger and Wilhelm Kühlmann [Berlin; Boston: De Gruyter, 2011], 15).

55 τῇ τῶν δεικνυμένων θεωρίᾳ προσανέχειν μόνῃ (PG 66.401).

56 Theodore of Mopsuestia, *Commentary on the Twelve Prophets*, 251.

57 Theodore in his opening comments on Nah 1:1 (ibid., 248 [PG 66.401]).

58 My literal translation, with the main verb translated as a passive (not a middle), while the dative of *theōria* is translated adverbially or as a manner (cf. TLG 4135.013 fragment 112, column 1, lines 15–17). Kalantzis has it, "For, clearly, whoever sees that One through this One, is clearly led to see because of the

likeness" (Kalantzis, *Theodore of Mopsuestia: Commentary on the Gospel of John*, 104). Kalantzis's translation flows better, but does not underscore as strongly the necessity of *theōria* as perception of the deity of Christ.

[59] Theodore of Mopsuestia, *Commentary on the Twelve Prophets*, 329 (PG 66:505).

[60] Similarly, Theodore comments on John 1:32, "John the Baptist sees the Holy Spirit as a dove according to some spiritual vision or discernment (*theōria*) as did the prophets. Others present did not perceive because they were not spiritually enabled" (TLG 4135.013 fragment 14, lines 2–3; cf. Kalantzis, *Theodore of Mopsuestia: Commentary on the Gospel of John*, 51–52).

[61] Ibid., 118 (italic is in the original as emphasizing the biblical text). The translation of the neuter pronoun as "it" does not display in Theodore a low view of the Holy Spirit as the Third Person of the Trinity but perhaps a zealousness by the translator to align with the Greek.

[62] If the apostles who walked with Jesus could not perceive that he is God without a work of the Holy Spirit and the completion of Jesus' work on the earth, how can any other interpreter hope to perceive Christ as God in life or in the Bible without the Holy Spirit? For a comparison of the methods of theology and exegesis in a representative Antiochene (Theodore) and Alexandrian (Cyril of Alexandria) from their commentaries on the Gospel of John cf. Luigi Fatica, *I commentari a "Giovanni" di Teodoro di Mopsuestia e di Cirillo di Alessandria: Confronto fra metodi esegetici e teologici* (Roma: Institutum Patristicum Augustinianum, 1988), 6, 7, 13, 70, 129, 174, 285, 288.

[63] TLG includes ten Greek sources for Theodoretus (of the geographic epithet Cyrrhensis) which contain his commentaries on forty-four books of the Bible.

[64] E.g., see Theodoret's comments on Ps 40:3; 64:7–8; Ezek 20:40–42; 26:15–16; and 39:23–24.

[65] E.g., for Moses in Theodoret's comments on question 68 for Exod in Theodoret of Cyrus, *The Questions on the Octateuch: On Genesis and Exodus*, 337.

[66] Hill, *Commentary on the Psalms, 1–72*, 134–135 (PG 80.992–993).

[67] In the context Theodoret discusses the impiety of the Jews not only in pre- and postexilic times, but also in Theodore's own day—who refuse to see Jesus Christ in the Scriptures as an example of such lack of preparation for discernment (Hill, *Commentary on the Psalms, 73–150*, 54 [PG 80.1525]).

[68] Ibid., 54n8. Later Hill claims that generally for Theodoret to "to grasp their [the Psalms] fully meaning, *theoria* is required, as the verb here indicates." The verb there in Theodoret's *Commentary on Psalms* 150:6 is θεωροῦμεν (ibid., 374–375n7 [PG 80.1997.7]).

[69] Hill, *Commentary on the Psalms, 73–150*, 51 (PG 80.1520). *Contra*, Theodore who sees this Psalm as David "foretelling the people's return from Babylon" and what state of heart brought them there to begin with (Hill, *Theodore of Mopsuestia: Commentary on Psalms 1–81*, 1113, 1119–1121).

[70] Furthermore, it can be argued from the research on Antiochene *theōria* by Heinrich Kihn that "by *allegoria* [ἀλληγορία] the Antiochenes meant 'arbitrary exegesis,' whereas *theōria* drew a distinction between allegory and the justified

higher sense" (Nassif, "The 'Spiritual Exegesis' of Scripture," 440. Nassif translates and cites from Heinrich Kihn, "Über θεωρία und ἀλληγορία nach den verloren hermeneutischen Schriften der Antiochener," *Theologische Quartalschrift* 20 [1880]: 536; cf. Perhai, "Antiochene *Theoria* in the Writings of Theodore and Theodoret," 159–176).

71 Theodoret—finding encouragement in the translation from Symmacus "your temple, which is *above* Jerusalem" (instead of "your temple *in* Jerusalem")—links the temple of verse 29 with Jesus' humanity from Ephesians 1:21.

72 Hill notes, "Theodoret in this psalm and almost consistently throughout the whole Commentary is anxious to take an eschatological and at times anagogical interpretation, seeing the psalmist's words realized at a later stage—*provided the reader follows the requisite process of θεωρία* (occurring here in verb form, as often). . . . As in his preface, he implies here that many fail to achieve it" (Hill, *Commentary on the Psalms, 1–72*, 391n41, emphasis mine).

73 Ibid., 221; *PG*, 80.1124.42. The verb for "illumined" is a present, passive, participle of φωτίζω.

74 Hill, *Commentary on the Psalms, 73–150*, 153–154.

75 Hill, *Commentary on the Psalms, 1–72*, 272 (PG 80.1205.39–47).

76 Apparently because David is seen as a prophet and Jesus made so much use of the Psalms to point to his day or himself (Quentin F Wesselschmidt, *Psalms 51-150* [Downers Grove, Ill.: InterVarsity, 2007], xvii–xix); cf. Acts 2:30. Furthermore, Viciano notes that the Antiochenes "read the Bible not just as a literal book but also as a God-inspired text θεόπνευστος (2 Tim 3:16) so that its own and unmistakable quality is manifested. With this quote out of 2 Timothy's letter Diodore opens his commentary on the Psalms because they are a book full of instruction (*Unterweisung*). David uses, through historical example, moving the reader of the Psalms to read them with him and in so doing fulfilling the especially high standard of all in the teaching office of all the prophets" (Albert Viciano, "Das formale der antiochenischen Schriftauslenung," in *Stimuli: Exegese und ihre Hermeneutik in Antike und Christentum: Festschrift für Ernst Dassmann* [ed. Georg Schöllgen and Clemens Scholten; Münster: Aschendorffsche, 1996], 388). So even the Psalms were deemed prophetic because they are inspired, thus instructive. And how could they be instructive unless they refer not only to their own time but others' as well?

77 Hill comments: "Theodoret is returning to his original principles in this closing hermeneutical review. He can be satisfied he has not devoted the bulk of his commentary to ancient history. While admitting the validity of looking for a historical application, he has not allowed this to be made exclusively of the history of the Jews but has encouraged his readers to look for another level of meaning (not κατὰ ἀναγωγήν, as Chrysostom would say, but τροπικώτερον). *And as an Antiochene he recognizes in this distinction of levels of meaning in a psalm text the process of θεωρία* (his final verb here being θεωρέω)" (Hill, *Commentary on the Psalms, 1–72*, 272n14, emphasis mine). In this observation Hill switches freely between the terms "application" and "meaning."

78 But while Philo uses τροπικώτερον, translated "metaphorically" (or "more figuratively") regularly in his writings, this term is a *hapax legomena* in Theodoret's extant writings (Peder Borgen, Kåre Fuglseth, and Roald Skarsten, *The Works of Philo: Greek Text with Morphology* [Bellingham, Wash.: Logos Research Systems, 2005], passim). A search for τροπικώτερον in *all* of Theodoret's extant writings compiled in the TLG database (not just the ten exegetical works) reveals PG 80.1204.44 as the only location of the term. Theodoret does, however, use the term τροπικῶς (meaning "figuratively" or "in a figurative sense") 129 times in all the TLG sources and all but one of them are in his commentaries. Figurative interpretation is defined herein as an explanation of a passage that assumes or understands the word or phrase not in its plain or literal sense, but as representing something else. Some would argue that the literal sense *includes* the figurative if that is the author's intent, and thus tend to only call figurative interpretation *mis*interpretation.

79 Theodoret of Cyrus, *Commentary on the Song of Songs* (trans. Robert C. Hill; Brisbane [Australia]: Centre for Early Christian Studies Australian Catholic University, 2001), 9, 12, 23. There is in the public domain one other translation of Theodoret's *Commentary on the Song of Songs* from an unknown translator, though several editorial notes throughout refer to "Parkhurst" (e.g., Theodoret, *Song of Songs*, 15).

80 Theodoret of Cyrus, *Commentary on the Song of Songs*, 24 (PG 81.32–33).

81 He uses Ezekiel 16–17 as an example of OT allegory demanding allegorical interpretation in his preface (ibid., 25–28 [PG 81.33–41]).

82 Cf. Ibid., 57.

83 Ibid., 21.

84 Ibid., 21–22; cf. 33.

85 Ibid., 33; *PG*, 81.49. Though Theodoret first surveys the songs of David and others in the OT comparing them with this one song of Solomon's, he then turns to themes of general delivery, then delivery from the devil, and adoption, that is "to designate and make us His Bride." And so Theodoret concludes the book is titled "Song of Songs" because it teaches "us the highest forms of the goodness of God, and the most inward and secret things, and revealing to us the most holy mysteries of the Divine philanthropy" (Theodoret, *Song of Songs*, xv–xx). If one understands Song of Songs typologically, then these are themes perhaps latent to its text, but certainly native to the NT text.

86 Thus he treats the text of the Song as purely prophetic, messianic allegory, rather than as typology.

87 Ibid., 2–3. He cites Hos 2:19–20 and Prov 8:11 in this context. For other examples of antecedent theology see ibid., 17n2.

88 He supports this with Col 2:9 as well as Isa 11:1–2.

89 Theodoret, *Song of Songs*, 6–7. Is this a more Antiochene historical approach, or a reference to Jews contemporary to Theodoret's readers? Apparently contemporary Jews, for according to Theodoret, she cultivated her former vineyard "before the Christian Faith." That is, apparently before she embraced the Christian faith.

[90] And in Song 1:9 the Pharaoh is for Theodoret, "the persecutor of our nature, our wicked and common enemy," namely, the devil. This devil the Bridegroom "drowned in the sacred waters of Baptism. Therefore He says, *My steed*, which I used when I plunged into the sea the chariots of Pharaoh, and set thee at liberty" (ibid., 9). His text reads "Unto a steed, well yoked with Me; In Pharaoh's chariot, I thee will, O My love compare" (ibid., 8). The ESV reads "mare" instead of "steed." The desire to maintain a grammatical explanation for "my" strains the credulity of the interpretation and the allegorical interpretation apparently keeps Theodoret from making reference to 2 Chronicles 1:17. The MT and ESV excludes me or my.

[91] Theodoret, *Song of Songs*, 13n3.

[92] Ibid., 25n1.

[93] This is an allusion to Gal 4:26 (ibid., 25).

[94] Ibid., 35n2; *PG*, 81.140.23–27.

[95] "You can also gain a different insight [*theōria*] from the sections in the middle: we see many ranks also among the saved, one of virgins, one of ascetics, one of those drawing the yoke of marriage, and of the affluent," etc. (Theodoret of Cyrus, *Commentary on the Song of Songs*, 84–85 [PG 81.144–145]). Cf. his continuing comments on pomegranates and contemplation (*theōria*) in Ibid., 102 (PG 81.181.8).

[96] Theodoret of Cyrus, *Commentary on the Song of Songs*, 105; cf. *PG*, 81.188.7. Hill translates *theōria* here as "fuller sense" but it seems unnecessary.

[97] TLG, 4089.008, translation mine. All of this follows in his comments in the latter part of Isaiah 12:6 on the verb ὑψώθη (aor. ind. pass. 3rd sg. from ὑψόω, to lift high, to raise up [LSJ, 1910]).

[98] "Now, he accords him the vision near water to imply that salvation of all people, and to suggest the knowledge of God by regeneration through water that would come to the devout." This appears to be an example of a non-literal/spiritual interpretation (PG, 81.820.45; cf. Robert C. Hill, tran., *Theodoret of Cyrus: Commentaries on the Prophets: Commentary on the Prophet Ezekiel*, vol. 2 (Brookline, Mass.: Holy Cross Orthodox Press, 2007), 35, 292n6; PG 81.821.17; cf. Hill, *Commentary on the Prophet Ezekiel*, 2:36. Cf. comments on Ezek 1:26 in PG 81.832.40; Ezek 3:22 in PG 81.852.28; and Ezek 8:3 in PG 81.881.36.)

[99] PG 81.852.28; Hill, *Commentary on the Prophet Ezekiel*, 2:54; cf. 2:296n12.

[100] PG 81.904.17–28; cf. Hill, *Commentary on the Prophet Ezekiel*, 2:83. Theodoret cites Matt 5:8 "Blessed are the pure in heart, for they shall see God" to support his appeal. Theodoret uses the term *theōria* similarly twice in Exodus, question 60 (answering why God had them construct a tabernacle). "Since the people of that time [the Exodus] were quite materialistic and incapable of attaining to spiritual realities, the Lord, in his great wisdom, devised a way of helping them through physical symbols. We, on the contrary, understand by the declaration [λόγιον] contemplation [*theōria*] of the intelligible, and by the shoulder cape the practice of virtue. We take the close fit of the declaration and the shoulder cape as the harmony of faith and virtuous behavior and understand the prior donning of the shoulder cape and the subsequent clasping of it to the declaration to

signify that virtuous behavior is the foundation of contemplation" (Theodoret of Cyrus, The Questions on the Octateuch: On Genesis and Exodus, 325, lines 158 and 165). The Greek text Theodoret works from uses the term λόγιον (declaration) where the MT has חֹשֶׁן (breastplate).

101 See Theodore's commentary on Nahum 1:1 above.

102 For a far more rigorous process of purification in order to achieve a mystical *theōria* from a Syrian contemporary of Theodoret see David Allen Michelson, "Practice Leads to Theory: Orthodoxy and the Spiritual Struggle in the Word of Philoxenos of Mabbug (470–523)" (Ph.D. diss., Princeton University, 2007). I am indebted to Jean Michelson, the Circulation Coordinator at Huntington University library for this connection.

103 Hill, *Commentary on the Prophet Ezekiel*, 2:262.

104 E.g., PG, 81.1356.35; 81.1493.32.

105 Ibid., 81.1384.24; cf. Hill, Theodoret of Cyrus: Commentary on Daniel, 140–141.

106 Robert C. Hill, trans., Theodoret of Cyrus: Commentary on The Letters of St. Paul (2d ed.; Brookline, Mass.: Holy Cross Orthodox Press, 2007), 169–170 (PG 82.736). Theodoret, like most in his day (besides the Arians and those who followed Origen) believes that Paul wrote Hebrews.

107 What kind of insight and where does it come from? Is it simply a matter of human contemplation? Or does Theodoret affirm a perception that comes by a gift of the Holy Spirit as Theodore does? See for an answer Theodore's comments on John 14:17 above.

108 Hill, Theodoret's Commentary on the Letters of St. Paul, 178, 181 (PG 82.752.31, 82.757.14).One may also ask Theodoret, from where comes faith?

109 "The Law required a red heifer to be sacrificed, and the high priest to take some of its blood and sprinkle the mercy seat seven times with his finger. Burning the heifer itself outside the camp, they took the ashes and with them purified thosepeople called impure. This acted as a type of the saving passion: the word red here means the body from Adam in the Hebrew language; he was fixed to the cross outside the gate; his blood purifies our souls; in place of the dust we have the life giving body" (Hill, *Theodoret's Commentary on the Letters of St. Paul*, 2:194–195 [PG 82.781.41–43]).

110 Typology or type is generally defined here as that, which "at least ties an event, a person or a thing to another event, person or thing within the framework of historical revelation." Paul Feinberg rightly notes that some view types as meaning outside a passage read into it (and thus not exegesis), while others see it as the primary means of linking the OT and NT (some seeing it different from and other similar to allegory. The former see a later writer describing "events in salvation history in light of OT events" while the latter are more inclined to a spiritual interpretation locating the fuller meaning). Still others view types as "intended by OT writers" and "discernible by historical-grammatical principles of hermeneutics." Thus typology includes "historical correspondence," "escalation," and certainly "divine intent" (and some would add divine "designation") between type and antitype (Paul D. Feinberg, "Hermeneutics of

Discontinuity," in Continuity and Discontinuity: Perspectives on the Relationship Between the Old and New Testaments: Essays in Honor of S. Lewis Johnson, Jr., ed. John S. Feinberg (Westchester, Ill.: Crossway, 1988), 120–121. This definition is held, despite the claims of some that the ancients did not distinguish between allegory and typology (e.g., Peter Williamson, Catholic Principles for Interpreting Scripture: A Study of the Pontifical Biblical Commission's the Interpretation of the Bible in the Church [Roma: Pontificio Istituto Biblico, 2001], 194). For more on these distinctions see Perhai, "Antiochene Theoria in the Writings of Theodore and Theodoret," 59–76 and the discussion of Gal 4:24 at the end of this article.

[111] 303,980 words for Theodore versus 891,901 for Theodoret as determined from analysis on the TLG digital database. While the entire TLG database of sources for Theodore is used in this study (which includes 9000 words in three non-commentary sources), Theodoret's non-commentary TLG sources with an additional 341,000 words is excluded from the study.

[112] Theodore uses the term *theōria* 15 versus 79 instances for Theodoret in the extant sources of TLG as discussed above.

[113] Theodore uses the term *theōreo* 36 versus 121 instances for Theodoret in the extant sources of TLG.

[114] Heisler makes note of this distinction, while not specifically commenting on how Theodore and Theodoret used *theōria* (Jeanne M. Heisler, "Gnat or Apostolic Bee: A Translation and Commentary on Theodoret's Commentary on Jonah" [Ph.D. diss., Florida State University, 2006], 15). Viciano, reviewing the19th century research of H. Kihn, F. A. Specht, L. Pirot and H. B. Swete summarizes that "Theodoret uses the same hermeneutic as Theodore. He recognizes very similar linguistic and theological questions. . . . However, these researchers unanimously emphasize Theodoret's originality . . . because when interpreting the OT he combines Antiochene θεωρία with the allegorical method" (Viciano, "Das formale der antiochenischen Schriftauslenung," 374).

[115] Mansi, ix, 225–227 cited in Quasten, Patrology, 3.406; cf. Theodoret of Cyrus, Commentary on the Song of Songs, 7n22; Henry Barclay Swete, "Theodorus of Mopsuestia," in A Dictionary of Christian Biography, Literature, Sects and Doctrines (ed. William Smith and Henry Wace; London: John Murray, 1887), 4:940; and Adolf Von Harnack, History of Dogma (electronic ed.; Grand Rapids: Christian Classics Ethereal Library, 2005), 129–130n329, http://www.ccel.org/ccel/harnack/dogma3.html).

[116] Rowan A. Greer, trans., Theodore of Mopsuestia: Commentary on the Minor Pauline Epistles (Atlanta, Ga.: SBL, 2010), 113.Scholars argue over the meaning of ἱστορία ("history" versus "narrative"). Either meaning is possible (LSJ, 842). But the question of whether Theodore was talking about history as events that really took place seems moot, since he follows the term ἱστορία with the phrase "what happened long ago." Cf. discussion above on ἱστορία.

[117] "Theodoret's [extensive] correspondence furnishes statements that enable us to date the Pauline Commentary to the mid-440s" when he had been a bishop for

approaching 25 years (Hill, *Theodoret's Commentary on the Letters of St. Paul*, 1:2).

[118] Hill, *Theodoret's Commentary on the Letters of St. Paul*, 17. Ἀλληγορούμενα εἶπεν ὁ θεῖος Ἀπόστολος, ἀντὶ τοῦ, Καὶ ἑτέρως νοούμενα. Οὐ γὰρ τὴν ἱστορίαν ἀνεῖλεν, ἀλλὰ τὰ ἐν τῇ ἱστορίᾳ προτυπωθέντα [aor ptc pss nom/acc pl from προτῠπόω; LSJ, 1537] διδάσκει (PG 82.489.45–48). Whether Theodoret sees this as a higher sense, he does not say. He only states that in Paul's use "it is to be understood differently" (ἑτέρως νοούμενα).

[119] PG, 82.492.42–45; Hill, Theodoret's Commentary on the Letters of St. Paul, 18.

[120] Christoph Schäublin, who writes a seminal work on Antiochene exegesis *Untersuchungen zu Methode und Herkunft der antiochenischen Exegese*, is definitive that when Paul uses the phrase ἅτινά ἐστιν ἀλληγορούμενα he means typology (Christoph Schäublin, "The Contribution of Rhetorics to Christian Hermeneutics," in Handbook of Patristic Exegesis: The Bible in Ancient Christianity [ed. Charles Kannengiesser; Leiden; Boston: Brill, 2004], 1:162n50). For a suggestive essay on the modern use of Antiochene rhetoric see Lauri Thurén, "John Chrysostom as a Modern Rhetorician," in *Rhetorics and Hermeneutics: Wilhelm Wuellner and His Influence*. Emory Studies in Early Christianity, ed. James D. Hester and J. David Hester (New York: T&T Clark, 2004), 218–240.

[121] Even Robert Hill (who often translates *theōria* as "higher sense" in both Theodore and Theodoret's works) affirms *theōria* as integral to Theodoret's hermeneutic. "Theodoret is brought at this early state by Hosea's marriage to lay out (with Cyril's help) Antioch's terminology for its hermeneutical approach to biblical texts. It is essential to recognize the purpose, *skopos*, of the text whether a simple narrative or one that is but an outline, *skia* [σκιά], foreshadowing the reality. Instead of having recourse to allegory, one should turn to discernment, *theōria*, of what is recounted or—in the case of Hosea's contemporaries— observed as happening before their eyes" (Robert C. Hill, trans., Theodoret of Cyrus: Commentaries on the Prophets: Commentary on the Twelve Prophets [Brookline, Mass.: Holy Cross Orthodox Press, 2006], 301n8). It is unfortunate that the original Greek version of Theodore's commentary on Galatians is not extant. His comments on Gal 2:25–30 from the Latin are translated several times as "discern" or "perceive" but there is no way to be sure that is a translation of the Greek. The texts read: "And if their [the allegorists'] view is true and what is written does not preserve an account of what really happened but points to something else profound and that must be understood intellectually—something spiritual, as they want to say, which they can *discern* since they are themselves spiritual people—where have they acquired this knowledge?"; and "He [Paul] wants to demonstrate that Christ's dispensation is greater than that of the law and that our righteousness should be *perceived* as far more excellent than that found in the law" (Greer, *Theodore of Mopsuestia: Commentary on the Minor 0Pauline Epistles*, 115, 117, emphasis mine).

[122] "The commentary of Theodoret of Cyr on St. Paul, strongly dependent on that of Chrysostom, has been preserved for us in its entirety in a continuous tradition

from the time of the early church, probably because Theodoret was viewed as a kind of synthesis or high point of Greek exegesis by later generations. Composed in the decades immediately preceding the Council of Chalcedon, that is, between A.D. 420 and 450, it is dry, scholarly and periphrastic. He is the *archrepresentative of Antiochene exegesis with its emphasis on a literal, rather than allegorical*, interpretation of the biblical salvation history and with the use of typological figurative explanations of passages in order to link the Testaments in a scheme of prophecy and fulfillment. . . . He demonstrated a remarkable concern for sorting out the chronological course of Paul's work. Each commentary on one of the epistles is preceded by a preface that discusses its setting and unifying themes" (Peter Gorday, *Colossians, 1–2 Thessalonians, 1–2 Timothy, Titus, Philemon*, ACCS NT 9 [Downers Grove, Ill.: InterVarsity, 2000], xxi, emphasis mine; cf. Guinot, *L'Exegésè de Théodoret de Cyr*, 71–76; and idem, "Theodoret of Cyrus: Bishop and Exegete," 163–193).

[123] Nassif, "Antiochene 'Theoria' in John Chrysostom's Exegesis."

[124] Schor, "Theodoret on the 'School of Antioch'," 522. Schor speaks in the context of Antiochene christological terminology, but we apply the same principle to exegetical terminology.

[125] Nassif, "Antiochene 'Theoria' in John Chrysostom's Exegesis," 212, 157.

The Comentary of St. Ephrem the Syrian

[1] St. Ephrem is commemorated twice in the liturgical calendar of the Armenian Church—once on the Saturday closest to January first, and the second time on the Saturday closest to October 26. See also Hovhanessian, "The Commentaries on the Letters of Paul Attributed to Ephrem the Syrian in Armenian Manuscripts," *The Harp: A Review of Syriac and Oriental Studies* XXIV (2009): 311–327. On the popularity pof the saitn among the Armenians see also, Abp. Norayr Bogharian, *Cisagitutiwn* [Liturgy] (New York: St. Vartan Press, 1990), pp. 8–9.

[2] See, Vahan Hovhanessian, "A Medieval Armenian Scholion on the Catholic Epistles" in *Exegesis and Hermeneutics in the Churches of the East*, Vahan Hovhanessian (ed.), (New York: Peter Lang, 2009), p. 125.

[3] For an extensive introruction to this apocryphal correspondence see Vahan S. Hovhanessian, *Third Corinthians: reclaiming Paul for Christian orthodoxy* (New York: Peter Lang, 2000).

[4] Joseph Schäfers, *Evangelienzitate in Ephräm des syrers commentar zu den paulinischen schriften* (Freiburg, 1917).

[5] Joseph Molitor, *Der Paulustext des Hl. Ephräm* (Rome, 1938).

[6] *êñµáÛÝ °÷ñ»ÙÇ ÊáñÇ ²ëáñõáÛ Ø³ï»Ý³·ñáÃÇõÝù* [Writings of Saint Ephrem Khori the Syrian], in four volumes, (Venice, 1836), henceforth, '*Commentary.*'

[7] *Ø»ÏÝáÃ³ÇõÝ âáñ»·ï³ë³ÝÇ ÂÕÃáÛ äÕÃáëÇ* [Commentary on the Fourteen Letters of Paul], *Commentary*, vol. 3, (Venice, 1836).

[8] *S. Ephraemi Syri Commentarii In Epistolas D. Pauli* (Venice, 1893).

9   The introduction describes the manuscript as 'a copy of a commentary on the Epistles written with the old *Bolorgir* script in AD 999, by a certain Simeon Vartabed in the Arcrun region during the reign of King Gagik the son of Ašot.' *Commentary*, vol. 1, p. 9.

10   Bzomar, Lebanon, MS 437; San Lazzaro, Venice, MSS 1600, 1604, 1609, 1612, 1614 and 1619; St. James, Jerusalem, MSS 1A, 234 and 1284; Matenadaran, Armenia, MSS 472, 1138, 1208, 3009, 3012, 3276, 3371, 3643, 3900, 4109, 4119, 5443, 5561, 5826, 7516, 7910 and 10161; Antelias, Lebanon, MSS 26 and 61; New Julfa, Iran, MSS 380 and 381.

11   *Commentary*, vol. 1, 8-9.

12   Vahan Hovhanessian, *Third Corinthians: Reclaiming Paul for Christian Orthodoxy* (New York, 2000), 10-12.

13   Hovhanessian, *Third Corinthians*, 11.

14   Sahak Jemjemian, *Mayr Cucak*, vol 8, cols. 399-408.

15   Sahak Jemjemian, *Mayr Cucak*, vol 8, cols. 417-422.

16   Sahak Jemjemian, *Mayr Cucak*, vol 8, cols. 451-464.

17   Sahak Jemjemian, *Mayr Cucak*, vol 8, cols. 469-472.

18   Sahak Jemjemian, *Mayr Cucak*, vol 8, cols. 473-478.

19   Bogharian, St. James, vol. 1, 1966, pp. 644-647.

20   Bogharian, St. James, vol. 4, 1969, pp. 476-478.

21   Tanielian, Antilias, 1984, p. 185-186.

22   Tanielian, Antilias, 1984, p. 268-270.

23   Vol. 1

24   Ibid

25   Ø»ÏÝáõÃÇõÝ, *Commentary*, vol. 3, (Venice, 1836), pp.

26   Refer to the chart published in Hovhanessian's *Third Corinthians*, pp. 139-145.

27   See, for example, the writings of the Aphraat (or Aphrahat). Josef Kerschensteiner, "Beobachtungen zum altsyrischen Actatext" *Biblica* 45 (1964), pp. 53-74.

28   Ø»ÏÝáõÃÇõÝ, *Commentary*, vol. 3, p. 116

29   Hovhanessian, *Third Corinthians*, pp. 1-3

30   J. K. Elliott, *The Apocryphal New Testament: A Collection of Apocryphal Christian Literature* (Ocford: Oxford University Press, 2005), pp. 379-380.

31   Sebastian P. Brock, 'The Poet as Theologian,' *Sobornost* 7 (1977), 243-250; P. Leloir, 'Symbolisme et parallélisme chez Saint Ephrem,' in *A la rencontre de Dieu. Mémorial Albert Gelin* (Lyon, 1961), 363-374; P. Tanios Bou Mansour, *La pensée symbolique de saint Ephrem le syrien* (Kaslik, Lebanon, 1988); Carmel McCarthy, 'Gospel Exegesis from a Semitic Church: Ephrem's Commentary on the Sermon on the Mount,' in *Tradition of the Text*, Gerard J. Norton and Stephen Pisano, eds, (Freiburg, 1991), 103-121; *St. Ephrem's Commentary on Tatian's Diatessaron*, Journal of Semitic Studies, Supplement 2, (Oxford, 1993), 14-23; and P. Yousif, 'Exegetical Principles of St. Ephraem of Nisbis,' *Studia Patristica* (Oxford, 1990), 296–302.

32   Kathleen McVey, ed., *St. Ephrem The Syrian* (New York, 1989), 43-44.

33   My translation of the Armenian text *Syrian* (New York, 1989), 43-44.

34   Hovhanessian, Third Corinthians, p. 78.

35   Hovhanessian, *Third Corinthians*, p. 77.

36   McCarthy, *St. Ephrem's Commentary*, 12.

37   C. W. Mitchell, M.A., *S. Ephraim's Prose Refutations of Mani, Marcion and Bardaisan*, vol. 2 (Oxford: Williams and Norgate, 1921). Se especially pages 143, 148, 160, 163, and 169 for St. Ephrem's proses against Bardaisan.

38   *Commentary*, vol. 3, 117-8. See also Hovhanessian, *Third Corinthians*, 126-127, E. Beck, 'Bardaisan und seine Schule bei Ephram,' *Le Muséon* 91 (1978), 271–333. In Galatians, the commentary mentions a certain heretic by the name of Simeon who was disturbing the community in Galatia. *Commentary*, vol. 3, 124-5.

39   McCarthy, *St. Ephrem's Commentary*, 17.

Bibliography

Baumstark, Anton. "Neue soghdisch-nestorianische Bruchstücke," *Oriens christianus. Hefte für die Kunde des christlichen Orients* 4 (N.S.) (1915): 123-28.

Boyce, Mary. *A Catalogue of the Iranian Manuscripts in Manichaean Script in the German Turfan Collection (Deutsche Akademie der Wissenschaften zu Berlin, Institut für Orientforschung, Veröffentlichung Nr. 45)*, (Berlin: Akademie Verlag, 1960).

Brock, Sebastian P. *The Bible in the Syriac Tradition (Gorgias Handbooks, Vol.* (Piscataway, NJ: Gorgias Press, 2006).

_____. "The Christology of the Church of the East in the Synods of the Fifth to Early Seventh Centuries: Preliminary Considerations and Materials," in *Aksum, Thyateira: A Festschrift for Archbishop Methodios of Thyateira and Great Britain* (ed. George Dion Dragas; London: Editorial Committee, 1985), 125-42.

_____. "The 'Nestorian' Church: A Lamentable Misnomer," *BJRL* 78 (1996): 23-35.

Bundy, David D. "The pseudo-Ephremian commentary on third Corinthians: a study in exegesis and anti-Bardaisanite polemic" in *After Bardaisan: studies on continuity and change in Syriac Christianity in honour of Professor Han J.W. Drijvers,* edited by G. J. Reinink, Alexander Cornelis Klugkist (Leuven: Uitgeverij Peeters en dép.oosterse Studies, 1999), pp. 51-64.

Childs, Brevard. *The Struggle to Understand Isaiah as Christian Scripture* (Grand Rapids: Eerdmans Publishing Company, 2004).

Dickens, Mark. "The Importance of the Psalmter at Turfan", In: *From the Oxus River to the Chinese shores: studies on East Syriac Christianity in China and Central Asia.* Li Tang, Dietmar W. Winkler (Eds.). Berlin: Lit, 2013), pp. 357-378.

Faros, Fr Philotheos, *Functional and Dysfunctional Christianity,* Holy Cross Orthodox Press, Brookline, Massachusetts, 1976.

Fairbairn, Donald. *Grace and Christology in the Early Church* (New York, New York: Oxford University Press, 2003).

Garrett, Duane A. *An Analysis of the Hermeneutics of John Chrysostom's Commentary on Isaiah 1-8 With An English Translation.* The Edwin Mellen Press, 1992, pp.123-5.

Hidal, Sten. "Exegesis of the Old Testament in the Antiochene School with its Prevalent Literal and Historical Method," in *Hebrew Bible/Old Testament: A History of Its Interpretation*, vol. 1/1 (Gottengen: Vandenhoeck & Ruprecht, 1996), 543-568.

Hovhanessian, Vahan. "A Medieval Armenian Scholion on the Catholic Epistles" in *Exegesis and Hermeneutics in the Churches of the East*, Vahan Hovhanessian (ed.), (New York: Peter Lang, 2009).

_____. *Third Corinthians: Reclaiming Paul for Christian orthodoxy* (New York: Peter Lang, 2000).

Hunter, Erica C. D. "The Church of the East in Central Asia," *BJRL* 78 (1996): 129-42.

Jullien, Christelle. *Controverses Des Chretiens Dans L'iran Sassanide* (Oakville, CT: David Brown Book Co., 2008).

Kennengiesser, Charles. "Biblical Exegesis and Hermeneutics in Syria," *Handbook of Patristic Exegesis: The Bible in Ancient Christianity*, vol. 2 (Leiden: Brill), 769-839 and 875-877; 885-918.

Molitor, Joseph. *Der Paulustext des Hl. Ephräm* (Rome, 1938).

Moreschini, Claudio and Norelli, Enrico. translated by Matthew J. O'Connell, "The Antiochene School," in *Early Christian Greek and Latin Literature: A Literary History* (Peabody, MA: Hendrickson Publishers, 2005).

Nassif, Bradley. "Antiochene Θεωρία in John Chrysostom's Exegesis" in *The Bible in the Eastern and Oriental Orthodox Churches*" ed. Vahan Hovanhessian (New York, New York: Peter Lang Publishers, 2009).

_____. "The 'Spiritual Exegesis' of Scripture: The School of Antioch Revisited," *Anglican Theological Review* (Vol. LXXV: 4, 1993), pp. 437-470.

_____. "Antiochene 'Theoria' in John Chrysostom's Exegesis" (Ph.D. diss., Fordham University, 1991).

Schäfers, Joseph. *Evangelienzitate in Ephräm des syrers commentar zu den paulinischen schriften* (Freiburg, 1917).

Schor, Adam M. "Theodoret on the 'School of Antioch': A Network Approach," Journal of Early Christian Studies 15 (Dec. 9, 2007): 517-562.

Sims-Williams, Nicholas. "Sogdian and Turkish Christians in the Turfan and Tun-Huang Manuscripts," in *Turfan and Tun-Huang, the Texts: Encounter of Civilizations on the Silk Route* (ed. Alfredo Cadonna; Firenze: Leo S. Olschki Editore, 1992), 43-61.

_____ and Hamilton, James. *Documents Turco-Sogdiens du IXe-Xe siècle de Touen-houang* (*Corpus Inscriptorum Iranicarum, Part II, Vol. III*) (London: School of Oriental and African Studies, 1990).

Sundermann, Werner, "Byzanz und Bulayïq," in *Iranian and Indo-European Studies: Memorial Volume of Otakar Klíma* (ed. Petr Vavroušek; Praha: Enigma Corporation, 1994), 255-64.

Tarazi, Paul. "The Book of Jeremiah and the Pentateuchal Torah" in Theodore G. Stylianopoulos, ed., *Sacred Text and Interpretation*, Holy Cross Orthodox Press, Brookline, Massachusetts, 2006, pp.7-36.

Vööbus, Arthur. *History of the School of Nisibis* (*Corpus Scriptorum Christianorum Orientalium 266/Sub. 26*) (Louvain: Secrétariat du Corpus SCO, 1965).

Zieme, Peter. "Notes on a Bilingual Prayer Book from Bulayık," in *Hidden Treasures and Intercultural Encounters: Studies on East Syriac Christianity in*

China and Central Asia (ed. Dietmar W. Winkler and Li Tang. Wien: LIT Verlag, 2009), 167-80.

_____. "A Cup of Cold Water," in *Jingjiao: The Church of the East in China and Central Asia* (ed. Roman Malek and Peter Hofrichter; Sankt Augustin: Institut Monumenta Serica, 2006), 341-45.

Index

•A•

Abraham, 10, 25, 59, 63, 90nn.42, 54
Ahab, 77, 80
Arab, 19, 22
Armenia, 71, 115n.10
Athanasius, 6, 103n.31
Azazel, 40

•B•

Babylon, 62, 107n.69
Baptism, 101n.14, 110n90
Beast, 43
Bodmer Papyrus, 72, 75
Byzantine(-ium), 19, 22, 67, 75n.3,
    86n.3

•C•

Catenae, 99n.2
Chalcedon(-ian), 6, 17, 50, 51, 100n.11,
    102nn.22, 26, 114n.122
Christology, 3, 83n.5, 87n.25, 91n.46
Condemn(-ation), 17, 51, 84n.5
Constantinople, 7, 17, 51, 102n.19
Covenant, 10, 11, 14, 60, 62, 104n.44
Creation, 57, 58, 73, 74
Creator, 24, 57
Creed, 23, 24, 30, 101n.14
Cyril of Alexandria, 107n.62
Cyril
        of Alexandria, 107n.62
        of Jerusalem, 15, 69, 85n.17

•D•

Daniel, 13, 52, 62, 63, 11n.105
David, the king, 14, 52, 53, 59, 73, 75,
    76, 104nn.43, 44
Death, 9, 84n.11
Desert, 19, 25, 26, 61
Diatessaron, 76, 115n.31

•E•

Edessa, 25
Ekklesia, 12
Euthalius, 69
Eutychus, 74
Exegesis, 2–4, 42, 44, 45, 47, 49, 50,
    59, 65, 83nn.2,3,4,6, 96nn.1, 4, 8,
    97n.35, 99nn.1, 3, 5, 100nn.5, 13,
    101n.13, 102n.27, 103n.39, 104n.44,
    105nn.45, 50, 106nn.50, 51,
    107nn.62, 70, 108n.70, 111n.110,
    113n.119, 114nn.122, 123, 125,
    114n.2, 115n.31,
Ezekiel, 8, 52, 57, 61–63,

•F•

Fast, 24, 45,
Fire, 9, 13, 46, 58
Freedom, 65, 76, 77
Fruit, 6, 7, 42

BIBLE IN THE CHRISTIAN ORTHODOX TRADITION

Vahan S. Hovhanessian, *General Editor*

This series aims at exploring and evaluating the various aspects of biblical traditions as studied, understood, taught, and lived in the Christian communities that spoke and wrote—and some continue speaking and writing—in the Aramaic, Arabic, Armenian, Coptic, Georgian, Romanian, Syriac, and other languages of the Orthodox family of churches. A particular focus of this series is the incorporation of the various methodologies and hermeneutics used for centuries in these Christian communities, into the contemporary critical approaches, in order to shed light on understanding the message of the Bible. Each monograph in the series will engage in critical examination of issues raised by contemporary biblical research. Scholars in the fields of biblical text, manuscripts, canon, hermeneutics, theology, lectionary, Apocrypha and Pseudepigrapha will have an enormous opportunity to share their academic findings with a worldwide audience. Manuscripts and dissertations, incorporating a variety of approaches and methodologies to studying the Bible in the Eastern and Oriental Orthodox traditions—including, but not limited to, theological, historiographic, philological and literary—are welcome. Further information about this series and inquiries about the submission of manuscripts should be directed to:

Acquisitions Department
Peter Lang Publishing, Inc.
29 Broadway, 18th floor
New York, NY 10006

To order books in this series, please contact the Customer Service Department:

(800) 770–LANG (within the U.S.)
(212) 647–7706 (outside the U.S.)
(212) 647–7707 FAX

or browse online by series:

www.peterlang.com